Bibliographic information published by the German National Library:

The German National Library lists this publication in the National Bibliography; detailed bibliographic data are available on the Internet at http://dnb.dnb.de .

Imprint:

Copyright © 2019 GRIN Verlag
Print and binding: Books on Demand GmbH, Norderstedt Germany
ISBN: 9783346075987

This book at GRIN:

https://www.grin.com/document/507926

Darko Lugonja

The concepts of Inter-Institutional Interoperability and Open Innovation

GRIN Verlag

GRIN - Your knowledge has value

Since its foundation in 1998, GRIN has specialized in publishing academic texts by students, college teachers and other academics as e-book and printed book. The website www.grin.com is an ideal platform for presenting term papers, final papers, scientific essays, dissertations and specialist books.

Visit us on the internet:

http://www.grin.com/

http://www.facebook.com/grincom

http://www.twitter.com/grin_com

UNIVERSITY OF ZAGREB

FACULTY OF ORGANIZATION AND INFORMATICS

PHD post graduate study of information sciences
Selected chapters from organization management

„The inter-institutional interoperability concept and open innovation contribution to organization culture and new paradigm development"

Pilot research paper upon the multiple case study

Darko Lugonja

Abstract

Information Communication Technology (ICT) ensures the key support to Sustainable Interoperability (SIO), Open Innovation, Internet of Things (IoT), Enterprise Resource Planning (ERP) and Enterprise Architecture (EA). SIO and ICT have mutually beneficial and complementary impact. The concept of sustainable inter-institutional interoperability (I3O) and network connectivity ensures further mutual development and continued contribution of EA and SIO, particularly in the public administration. The new Internet and open innovation are opening the possibility of further IT development in different areas, based on the multiple networks contribution and resource sharing. SIO need to be supported with sound communication, standardization and organization culture.

Keywords

Information Communication Technology (ICT), Interoperability (IO), Sustainable Interoperability (SIO), InterInstitutional Interoperability (I3O), Internet of Things (IoT), Open Innovation (OI), Enterprise Resource Planning (ERP), Enterprise Architecture (EA)

1 Introduction

This work aims for contribution to the concept of sustainable interoperability (SIO) establishment and its implementation, featuring the open innovation (OI), sustainable IT systems (SITS), as well as their integration and support to the sustainable information society (SIS) further development. That may have a significant impact to public administration. The public administration (government, agencies, ministries, state enterprises and institutions) represent more than 20% of the EU employees, there is a need to consider the ICT and OI impact to the further public sector and social development. The concept of I3O and this paper, as well as the future research is based on the development and its contribution to SIO development, given the key influences of the following elements:

• SIO development with regard to EA and organizational specifics,

• SITS (Sustainable Information Technology Systems),

• IO / EA (Interoperability / Enterprise Architecture),

• SIS (Sustainable Information Society).

Contemporary business and science are witnessing growing number of networks and communications locally and globally, through the new internet (IoT and related areas), so the public institutions networks' growing number may indicate the trend. Communication and connection are sine qua non for each business and enterprise, organization, unit, as well as for each individual.

1.1 The Background and Research Motivation

Contemporary business, ICT studies and projects, national and cross-national programs and activities, are stressing the interoperability, in order to ensure systems' functionality and sustainability. As one of the critical points of enterprise and public administration functionalities, interoperability ensures communication functioning, but also enterprise development. Being employed for more than decade in public administration, in EU related activities, with sound experience of working in global enterprises, author dedicated its life and career to studies related to organizations, business, IT, communication and related areas. He confirmed his interest in organization and society development, interrelated and interdependent, so that influenced him to study the organization and ICT development. Accordingly, author considered his experiences in large organizations, public administration and large private enterprises, approving the need for the ICT development, sustainable implementation and adoption, as well as interoperability leading to sustainable information society development.

Lack of adoption, acknowledgment, recognition and low level of interoperability are described and studied across the academic and business networks and societies. Yet, there is a growing need for the concept that will contribute to sustainable interoperability and information society development. The I3O as a concept recognize interoperability issues in large systems, enterprises and public administration in general, various issues and improvement areas, as well as need for continuous development and open architecture incorporating new elements and restructuring. Interoperability influence to synergies and systems development, as well as further concepts, implications and consequences, is not developed enough to support the need for the new paradigm for the growing number of systems and networks incorporated. In order to ensure the contribution to concept and construct development, for the further research, author planned to conduct the research on the new concept and paradigm of I3O concept development need and its outcomes.

Public administration, following the society development, ICT development and its impact to society at all, is supportive to ICT adoption, implementation and its contribution to further SIS development, through various areas: e-government, e-citizen, state-aid programs supporting new educational programs. There are mutual influences and benefits to social development.

This paper aims for the I3O concept development, research and description, as well as its contribution to new paradigm development and implementation. A research that aims for I3O concept research has following goals:

1) Framework that ensure development and implementation of I3O concept,

2) Contribution and benefits from the I3O concept (stakeholders, contributors),

3) Development of I3O concept

In order to develop and test such a concept author considered previous experiences, relevant literature and studies upon the mentioned areas. According to his previous experience, he found interoperability development and its contribution to further sustainable information society development critical and motivational to pursue a study and a research upon this research topic. Considering a need for the concept that will ensure interoperability development, across the public administration, new paradigm adoption, as well as IT, open innovation and proactive policy, conducting in new environment, author appreciate articulation of such a concept and its further development, in order to be sustainable for eventual future research upon public administration architecture and support its adoption.

A growing number of research papers in this area lead author to consider the sources upon administration communication and development in turbulent changes. Author considered his professional and personal experiences relevant for the initiative and support for such a concept building, as the literature findings and contemporary business and science lead to conclusion that there is a growing need for it. Considering public administration across national and EU framework, their growth and development, strengths, weaknesses, opportunities and threats (SWOT), author found a need for the inititative and concept building to ensure instisional path for the adaptation of new technologies and sustainable information society development, towards mutually benefitial and supportive framework.

Systems strenghts are in large number of qualified, well educated experts employed, their connections, networking and system incorporation, financial and political power that enable and support policies implementation, their opportunities are their capacity and influence onto almost every of the processes in the contemporary society, potential for negotiation, absorbing and purchasing new ICT, organizational and science projects and solutions, so ability to influence the market, economy, society in general.

Yet, there are threats in vulnerability resulting from the complexity and lack of flexibility, adaptability and standards in certain organization levels, economical and political instabilities. Stressing their weaknesses, such as excessive complexity, growth and development, hard to plan, organize, integrate and develop, and there are growing needs for specific solutions. Those solutions need multidiscipline approach and open architecture for further development and adaptation to new environment changes.

Aiming for such a concept that will encircle various approaches and concepts incorporation, integration and keeping flexible platform for further development, author considered interinstitutional interoperability (I3O) concept. When considering the challenges leading to this idea, author was focused primarily to organization and capacity issues, adaptability, as well as lack of organizational culture that support the organizational change and improvement through interoperability development. There were various case studies, literature views and considered topics, related and relevant for the concept initiative and establishment.

Author considered the paradigm as critical, so to ensure exploring various concepts, as the political power plays the key role in the goals' setting, transformation into policies and strategies, programs and projects, leading to outcomes not always adequatelly and logically approved by arguments.

There is a strong need to considerate a research on the thesis that **the interoperability initiatives and activities depend on political and cultural issues in organizations, so changes aiming for the I3O concept development and incorporation need to be supported and in line with cultural changes.**

1.2 Referral databases search and definitions

This work is based upon several case studies selected upon its relevance and relation to future research, organization development area, establishment and implementation of I3O, OI, as well as ICT contribution to the development of a SIO and SIS. Following the search upon referral databases and relevant papers reviewing (WoS, Scopus, Inspec, IEEE/Xplore, Academic Source Complete, DOAJ, European Commission, Google Scholar and Citeseer), author considered the selected papers and studies case studies.

In order to develop an appropriate methodology and the concept, construct and research thesis, at first author planned to conduct a study upon the relevant litarature. After the relevant literature study author propose secondary data analysis (UN, EU and global institutions and organizations publications and data bases) and data analysis accordingly.

1.3 Definitions

Following to the need for clarification, author proposed a short definition set.

Enterprise Architecture (EA) - is mostly defined as a systematic approach that organizes and guides the design, analysis, planning and documentation of activities in the enterprise.

ERP - according to Sommer, ERP (Enterprise Resource Planning) represents a process-oriented management view with regard to organizational re-alignment. (IT Dictionary, 1993)

Internet of Things (IoT) - the network of physical objects that contain embedded technology to communicate and sense or interact with their internal states or the external environment.

Interoperability (IO) - is defined as "ability of a computer system to run application programs from different vendors, and to interact with other computers across local or wide-area networks regardless of their physical architecture and operating systems. Interoperability is feasible through hardware and software components that conform to open standards such as those used for internet". (Business dictionary, 2017)

Open Innovation was defined as the use of purposive inflows and outflows of knowledge to accelerate internal innovation, and expand the markets for external use of innovation, respectively.

Process IO - This kind of IO is achieved when human beings share a common understanding across the network, interact with business systems, and coordinate work processes.

Semantic IO - Dolin and Alschuler define it as "the ability to import a statement from another computer without prior negotiation and support your decisions, query data and business rules and continue to work reliably against those statements". (Dolin and Alschuler, 2010)

Technical IO allows data transfer from system A to system B, regardless of distance. This domain is independent and is not related to content. The information theory, which describes 100% reliable communication over a noisy channel, is the cornerstone of technical interoperability.

Semantic Web Technology - refers to the W3C vision of Web related data. Such technologies enable people to create data web warehouses, build dictionaries and write rules for data handling. Related data is enhanced by technologies such as RDF, SPARQL, OWL and SKOS. (W3, 2017)

Sustainability - The variety of definitions leads to the one that define the sustainability as the ability to sustain, maintain, support, or confirm entity in general. There are various explanations, linking it to a range of sciences and disciplines.

A System - A set of things that work together as part of a mechanism or interconnected network; complex entity

1.4 The I3O concept - multiple influences

The I3O concept, OI and their contribution to SIS development are interdependent, related to various influences, but author considered important to focus onto critical components considered, covered by following case studies and literature citing, as presented in figure 1.

Figure 1 presents the concept components, as well as its interdependency.

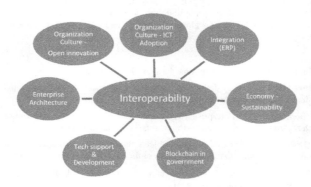

As there is similarity to star forms and correlation to space relations between stars, planets and various relations and objects, author presented I3O as a star relating to other stars, space objects and bodies.

2 Case study analysis upon the contribution of I3O and OI to the organization development

IO and EA are taking new importance in public administration, as well as the most of large systems. Large enterprises and public administration systems are oriented towards network development and their communication is strongly related to each aspect of interoperability. EU and European countries, as well as the most of developed countries have incorporated various strategies for interoperability development and implementation into national legal and political, as well as operational framework.

Regardless of initial success in strategies building and aligning political and institutional frameworks, many targets and plans were incompletely achieved, due to many challenges and issues standing as a barriers on the way to full interoperability systems. One of the key issues in reaching implementation success was that generally e-government efforts were in a lack of systems interoperability, adequate communication and integration, so to ensure the infrastructure development and progress, so the most of stakeholders became aware of the fact that interoperability and integration are complex and challenging aim. Since the public administration is oriented towards service providing and ensuring the public service systems, they are strongly focused onto communication, as well as integration and systems development. Accordingly, they support the integration of systems and activities extends to greater collaboration and integration between agencies, in order to ensure particular benefits.

2.1 Blockchain in government: Benefits and implications of distributed ledger technology for information sharing by Svein Ølnes, Jolien Ubacht, Marijn Janssen

Blockchain represents a range of general purpose technologies, so to exchange information and transact digital assets in distributed networks. *The core question addressed in this paper is whether blockchain technology will lead to innovation and transformation of governmental processes.*

Authors presented a critical assessment of the usually non-critically exaggerated blockchain technology benefits found in the literature and discuss their implications for governmental organizations and processes.

They suggested a shift from a technology-driven to need driven approach in which blockchain applications are customized to ensure a fit with administrative processes requirements and in which the administrative processes are changed due to technology benefit. Having sound governance models became a condition for realizing benefits. Based on a critical assessment they offered directions for further research into the potential benefits of BC applications in e-government and the role of governance of BC architectures and applications to comply with societal needs and public values.

Blockchain technology (BCT) is viewed is viewed as one of the most important general purpose technology trends that will influence business and society in the years to come, it has emerged as a potentially disruptive, general-purpose technology for companies and governments to support information exchange and transactions that require authentication and trust. It is quite a challenging task to define BCT, particularly from the viewpoint of virtual currency, Bitcoin blockchain, Ethereum blockchain, digitized tokens, smart deals, etc. In general, those terms are related with the common distributed "main book" or data distributed to many servers. Communication participants have the same data and a registry is a kind of database with transactions (or other data) stored in many places instead of one place (central server). (Janssens et. al 2017).

BCT itself stores the same information at different nodes and the information will only be added when the nodes have reached consensus. Previous information is stored and new information added to block, so this way ensured the traceability upon the previous and recently added information. This way of storing transaction is called a distributed ledger. Such an approach reduce the central actor role and risk of dependency, as well as other risks like the risk of manipulation or system failure as all nodes have the full information.

The purpose of BCT may be streched towards various ownership changes, important information storage and sharing, particularly the documents like certificates, licenses, government decisions and legislation. In general, BCT stored information represent transactional data like the ownership of land registry, birth and marriage certificates, vehicle registries, (business) licenses, educational certificates, student loans, social benefits and votes. BCT has the potential to provide benefits to government and society and can present the next step in e-government development, as they enable reduced costs and complexity, shared trusted processes, improved discoverability of audit trials and ensured trusted recordkeeping. Recently, the literature upon BCT was focused on the technology level, the technological challenges of using BCT for peer to peer (P2P) processes or the opportunities offered to redesign transaction and information exchange processes in the private domain. (Janssens et. al 2017).

Yet, critically less than significant number of literature and / or research was focused on BCT and its ability to address societal needs, as well as the potential of applications based on the BCT for governments explored in a systematic way. The vast majority of literature and research upon BCT was focused on potentials, benefits and critical differences to other relevant technologies and paradigms, ignoring the critical issues like implementation, trade-offs, limitations, materiality and governance aspects which might limit the possibilities. This paper authors ensured an overview of potential benefits, but also a critical review of pitfalls, challenges, providing space for government to manage and ensure BCT benefits to materialize. Paper aims is to contribute a more substantiated discussion about BCT in government by drawing the attention to aspects that are underemphasized and need more research, presenting a brief overview of the BCT, followed by the characteristics of BCT to governmental processes. They also discuss potential benefits that may be achieved by developing, running BCT implementation as part of government processes, followed by design options for different forms of BCT applications. Additionally, they discuss the implications and the possible roles of government organizations, in line with their social mandates and available design and implementation options, so to ensure that the BC applications deliver public value. In their conclusion they contribute to the research agenda on BCT in the public domain by presenting future research topics aimed at exploring the added value and to arrive at a better understanding of the consequences of BCT for governments.

2.2 Interoperability – cross border administration
"Cross-National Interoperability and Enterprise Architecture", by Gøtze et al

Gøtze et al have studied enterprise IO framework as a part of frameworks diversity, describing the part of various frameworks that may be established by each government, following their needs and activities. (Gøtze et al). Following the study upon the cross-national IO, the key challenges were based not only upon the IT and enterprise IO, but upon the set of framworks' diversities that enterprise IO systems and IT systems. Those frameworks were part of cross-national IO frameworks, so that leads to conclusion that mentioned systems are continuously growing in their complexity. Researchers described EA as "a plan, a strategic information base that can be used as a guideline for goals achievemet and a management process for understanding the business. Following the findings and studies, author defined EA as a systematic approach that organizes and guides design, analysis, planning, and documentation activities in an enterprise". (Gøtze et al., 2009)

When describing interoperability maturity, there is equal need to describe enterprise architecture maturity models, as equally complex system, as there are more complex issues, not only the observing or moving to the next level of categorized levels. "Cross-National Interoperability and Enterprise Architecture", as it provided a comprehensive overview of institutional interoperability at various levels, national and international, the level of maturity between the national IO activities of 13 countries, including the assessment of national EA programs and IO, to determine if they serve as important precursors for inclusion in interoperable interoperable co-operation. Governments adopted the EA as an e-government improvement instrument, to create a coherent approach to the e-government improving IO. EA is often viewed as a codified understanding that encompasses elements ranging from organization to infrastructure. The purpose is to close the gap between high policies of organization and implementation of low-level information systems. Important elements of EA are the framework, tools, principles, forms, core content and common services. EA is primarily product-oriented, while socio-political aspects often neglect. (Gøtze et al., 2009)

Authors presented EA future vision in "Beyond Alignment: Applying Systems Thinking in Architecting Enterprises", by pointing the enterprise "thinking" as a comprehensive view of how enterprises implement systematic thinking in EA, business transformation and strategic execution. They consider systematic thinking as a valuable way of thinking about sustainable entrepreneurship and how architecture works. Just like for IO, there are models and levels describing the evolution from initial awareness to systematically developed programs on the national level, EA also includes 4 levels: (0) awareness, (1) establishment, (2) operation and (3) value-adding. Recent e-government models were primarily focused to the information systems integration, vertical and horizontal, a complex system of activities implying institutions collaboration on various levels and platforms. EA programs and IO are ensuring collaborations, nationally and cross-nationally. (Gøtze et al., 2009)

Gotze et al study provided an analysis of cross-national IO collaboration in the governmental domain in an international perspective, for in this way to be able to measure the maturity levels of the collaborations. A study „found that national EA programs and national IO collaborations serve as important precursors for engaging in cross-national IO collaborations". Contemporary public administration, particularly on the national and cross-national level are oriented towards IO, featuring various maturity levels, as well as in EA program or national IO levels. Maturity of their cross-national, intraregional and global collaboration and IO is regurlarly on the higher level than the one at the national level. (Gøtze et al., 2009)

Recent studies and analysis have shown that human resource component is the critical one, particularly at the top management and leadership level as that area is closely related to decision making. This is more visible on the higher IO maturity levels, hence on the international and global levels. Political influence is the critical issue as many decisions on the top management are closely related to political issues. Political influence and its impact on the nations' collaborations may be categorised into a bipartition, one partition containing the member nations of EU and another partition containing everyone else. (Gøtze et al., 2009)

The rationale for such a division is that nations placed inside the EU may have one set of drivers for establishing the cross-national IO collaborations, while nations placed outside the EU may have another set of drivers. EU member states collaborations are policy driven by the implementation of the Internal Market (the free flow of workers, goods and services, etc.), supported by the IDABC program. Outside the EU it is believed that the initialisations of the cross-national IO collaborations are based on clear operational needs, not policy-based as in the EU. According to the collected data it is not possible to verify the claim, and it should therefore be exposed for further investigation in order to determine what implication, it has for the cross-national IO collaborations." (Gøtze et al., 2009)

Those conclusions are opening an area for research and studies upon political influence of the system and sustainable IO, as that aspect is the final point in making decisions upon the present and future collaboration. Multi-agent and variable influences are the basis for the further political influence onto basically technical operations and generating a circle of influences that may represent the grand challenge for each participant of the system. Given the situation of multilateral influences, as it is in the political environment, there are additional efforts needed for the development and establishment of political consensus and decision making with minimum political influence. Bilateral and multilateral collaborations and interoperability are plaftorm for their improvement, as EA and IO implementation leads to standardization and harmonization to the next level of communication and collaboration, therefore implementation is factically depending on the human resource issues. (Gøtze et al., 2009)

Being aware of those issues, EU political establishments, as well as scientific authorities contributed to establishement and development of „and thereby be recommended to use the EIF as the framework for cross-national interoperability collaborations, expects to provoke multilateral solutions, so this project is still under development, particularly the cross-national IO collaborations. In order to ensure measurability and traceability for EA and IO implementation, there are maturity levels, a range of EA maturity frameworks, applied one to the survey results. Gotze et al have presented „a range of interoperability frameworks and through a synthesis identified a possible way of measuring actual interoperability between entities, and finally placed the IO collaborations into a wider context and produced an IO collaboration maturity model. This model has been tested and produced the findings, and thereby it has proved its worth as a usable model. Even so, the maturity model may be exposed for further research and development for ensuring the adaption of ongoing progression of activities within crossnational IO collaborations ".There is strong focus on IO including compatibility of entities, procedures and equipment. In order to reach the planned IO level, each component, IT systems and procedures for each component need planned level of compatibility, in order to ensure planned activities. As interoperability became one of the strategic key issues in EU, there is growing number of governments and institutions that supported new solutions establishent and implementation, so to ensure e-government as a new guideline for new set of Pan-European e-Government Services.

IO and EA are often defined as a national and global priority, so each government have their program for EA and IO establishment, development, incorporation into strategies and programs, as well as implementation of such programs and schemes. (Gøtze et al., 2009)

When discussing challenges of those global trends and programs, one of the first complex issues is human resource, as there are not only lack in skilled staff and an adequate education, but also in the new systems of values and priorites adopted by employees. Those challenges are obvious, not only for private companies, but also for public administration and governments at all. EU administration defined human resource critical, particularly in the ICT sector, but also in management and leadership positions, as their support and new policies adoption is sine qua non. Lack of experts and lower level of cultural differences awareness, as well as other similar barriers lead to limited results and figures when considering outcome. There is another critical issue in funding such programs, as they take decades and large sum of activities, with minimal or zero (0) short term outputs and long term envisioned outcomes that are complex and not easily understandable. (Gøtze et al., 2009)

2.3 Interoperability across the EU
"Towards a Public Multilingual Knowledge Management Infrastructure for the European Digital Single Market ", by Peter Schmitz, Enrico Francesconi, Najeh Hajlaoui, Brahim Batouche

This paper was the case study choice for its relevance to the research and thesis development. There are various related topics, studies and connections that ensured author an insight into the study area. It was publicized by the Publications Office of European Union, Luxembourg and ITTIG-CNR, Florence, Italy, describing the Public Multilingual Knowledge Management Infrastructure (PMKI) ISA2 project first phase. PMKI aims to support the language technology industry, public administrations with multilingual tools, able to improve digital services cross border accessibility. It aims for a set of tools and facilities, based on Semantic Web technologies, for establishing semantic interoperability between multilingual lexicons. (Schmitz et al. 2017)

Authors conducted a study upon the data models for representing lexicons and recommendations for the PMKI service among the main data models. They have also discussed expected synergies with other programs of the EU institutions, systems interoperability and machine translation solutions. PMKI as the platform features interoperability as one of the main features, a platform that support multilingual tools development - machine translation, localization, search etc., and provide the machine translation tool, translation data as a factor of success to improve the quality mainly for underresourced languages. As cultural and linguistic diversities represent one of the key challenges, but at the same time, they are the key components and fundament of the European Union, so bridging the differences and connecting the cultures became one of the key priorities. Those issues and values need bridging to incorporate measures and activities that will protect those values, but also ensure a space of freedom, justice and democracy for EU citizens. (Schmitz et al. 2017)

EU economy benefit from exploring and bridging such barriers through globalization utilizing in the most appropriate way, through the creation of a Digital Single Market for the EU, as one of the leading priorities, so to provide better online access to digital goods and services, provide a supportive environment where digital networks and services as make "digital" as a growth driver. Public Multilingual Knowledge Infrastructure (PMKI), as a component and a pilot project launched within the ISA2 program, aimed to contribute solve issues of cross-border cooperation of Digital Single Market, particularly the language and semantic barriers. In order to build the Connecting Europe Facility Automated Translation (CEF.AT) platform - aims to create a set of tools and facilities, based on semantic Web technologies, aimed with multilingual tools in order to improve cross border accessibility of e-commerce solutions and public services. (Schmitz et al. 2017)

The key PMKI objective is to establish semantic interoperability between digital services, or to be more precise – to overcome the Internet language and technical barriers by creating the multilingual vocabularies and lexicons, and establishing links between them. so to support the enterprise digital systems in data exchange with unambiguous, shared meaning, supporting the accessibility of services and goods offered across the Internet.

The paper describes the PMKI project first phase, a feasibility study upon the implementation of mapping facilities and relations between multilingual lexicons based on semantic Web technologies. As PMKI objective is to implement a proof-of-concept infrastructure to expose and to harmonize internal (European Union institutional) and external multilingual lexicons, it aims for aligning them to facilitate interoperability. Furthermore, the project aims to create a governance structure to extend systematically the infrastructure by the integration of supplementary public multilingual taxonomies/terminologies. PMKI as a pilot project aims to check the feasibility and to prepare a road map to convert such proof of concept into a public service. (Schmitz et al. 2017)

In order to ensure the semantic interoperability of digital services, the need for such a platform has shown obvious and growing, particularly for the fact PMKI is a multilingual platform that can play the role of a hub to collect and to share language resources in standardised formats, providing domain specific terminologies alignments for developing domain specific translation systems (tender terminology, medical terminology, etc.). In addition such a platform may become a one window view or one-stop-shop for harmonized multilingual lex-icons repository at European level. Primarily, it aims for multilingual language resources harmonization, supporting their interoperability, and secondary, for integration of supplementary public multilingual taxonomies/terminologies in a standardized representation. Accordingly, there is a need for definition of the following requirements:

1) sophisticated standard representation used with respect to a
2) defined core data model (in case with extensions) under
3) an adequate architecture. (Schmitz et al. 2017)

Those requirements are analyzed and detailed in first analysis phases of the project:

- Analysis of existing relevant standards for the representation of lexicons that will be made available on the PMKI platform;
- PMKI core data model and extensions (based on the standard representation that is recommended as result of the previous analysis);
- Analysis of available platforms for managing lexicons. (Schmitz et al. 2017)

When selecting the most appropriate PMKI project standard, authors collected their requirements and referred them to the available standards for lexical resources and their enrichment, so in particular, they have analyzed SKOS, WordNet, Lemon and OntoLex. The collected requirements were associated to the type of lexical resources which PMKI aims to deal with and to the type of their possible lexical enrichment. In their analysis they have identified the PMKI requirements covered by the following resource types: (1) controller vocabularies, (2) glossaries, (3) lexicons, (4) thesauri, (5) taxonomies and (6) semantic networks, as listed in Tab. 1, where the second colon describes the projected requirements. (Schmitz et al. 2017)

2.4 The ICT Adoption

"The Contribution of ICT Adoption to the Sustainable Information Society", by Ewa Ziemba

Ziemba, E.,"The Contribution of ICT Adoption to the Sustainable Information Society". This paper was additional case study, relevant for the further research. The article describes the growing and ever more direct influence of adopting information technologies on the building of a sustainable information society and the application of new practices, with the aim of contributing to the improvement and enhancement of information society research and practice by examining and understanding the adoption of ICT in enterprises for the purpose of improvement and the development of a sustainable information society (SIS). The paper is based on a study that uses a quantitative approach to research how companies adopt ICT and how it affects different forms of sustainability and improves the development of a sustainable information society. (Ziemba, 2017)

Survey questionnaires were used for research and analysis, and data from 396 companies were collected for the purpose of understanding the correlation between adopting ICT and SIS. Research results show that the quality of ICT, management and information culture have a significant impact on SIS sustainability, while ICT spending does not have such an impact.

This study improves the research and practice of the information society by developing a model that demonstrates the dimensions of ICT adoption and the impact on different types of sustainability in the SIS. This is a research based on an appropriate methodological framework and concept, analysis of survey results, research and practical experience and new practices application and description. Data analyzes were carried out on 396 companies, based on the same, proposals for new practices and methodologies for further work on ICT adoption, new practices and impact on different types of sustainability in SIS. (Ziemba, 2017)

The study area is the management of information systems (MIS) and the development of a sustainable information society (SIS). The author gives a very good overview of the relevant literature with the most relevant and numerous references, and the research hypotheses are successfully placed. The research methods used were based on the research carried out in 396 companies. As a way of collecting data, a survey was conducted and an analysis of the survey results, and the conclusion is that ICT quality, management and information culture have a significant influence on SIS, while ICT spending does not have so much impact. (Ziemba, 2017)

The study helps to improve the research and practice of the information society by developing a model that demonstrates the dimensions of ICT adoption and the impact on different types of sustainability in the SIS. The article's conclusions are positive, with the remark that appropriate approaches and methodology are applied to the terms, objectives and circumstances. It is a combination of quantitative and qualitative research - the author analyzes the values and the quantity, intensity and practice of enterprises, based on literature analysis and own knowledge, experiences and acquired knowledge defines concept, construct and hypothesis, and further elaboration and data gathering takes place through research and survey, data analysis and research results, conclusions and guidelines. Analytical methods used have been relevant and author's experience in approaching and describing this problem is relevant. As a result of the previous research and the established differences in approach, the objectives of the research were set: Operationalization of SIS structures, ie adoption of ICT and sustainability in SIS; Empirical testing of SIS constructs and sub-constructs; Empirical Impact Assessment to Improve ICT Sustainability in the SIS. (Ziemba, 2017)

The construct of effective and efficient adoption of ICT implies a series of conditions and goals fulfilling, featuring the achievement of economic, social, environmental and political benefits. Based on the literature analysis, the author presents the adoption of information systems and the influence of 4 categories of factors, organizational, managerial, technological and information. The author states that Chen and colleagues examined the key factors of ecologically based decisions on adopting ICT. In their factor framework, four groups of factors are identified: support of the top management structure, state support, resource allocation, technological resources, and management and management of the overall organization. By analyzing articles and new findings in science and literature, it can be assumed that the adoption of ICT is a multi-dimensional construct that consists of expenditure on ICT, information culture, ICT and ICT quality management. (Ziemba, 2017)

Analyzing the ICT influence to the development of new practices and the stages of a SIS, author find useful its contribution to the science development, techniques, practices, as well as the paradigm of SIO, with a series of links that stimulate and interrelate but also as a thematic and methodological basis for further development. The development of ICT governance methods and practices as a contribution to the development of SIO and SIS is part of the new EU policy (Horizon 2020) but also the market necessity in the context of intense and continuous changes. The methodology and results presented, based on relevant research during and after this research, are the basis for further analysis and research, pointing to the significance and potential of this area. The literature demonstrates numerous quality references. (Ziemba, 2017)

Author used a literature study and quantitative approach upon the question how companies adopt ICT, how it affects sustainability and improves the SIS development. The study area is the management of information systems (MIS) and the development of a sustainable information society (SIS). The author gives an excellent relevant literature overview with the most relevant and numerous references, the research hypotheses were successfully set. The research methods used were based on the research carried out in 396 companies. (Ziemba, 2017)

A survey and an analysis of the survey results were conducted, and it lead to the conclusion that ICT quality, management and information culture have a significant influence on SIS, while ICT spending does not have such a significant impact. (Ziemba, 2017)

The study helps to improve the research and practice of the information society by developing a model that demonstrates the dimensions of ICT adoption and the impact on different types of sustainability in the SIS. The article's conclusions are positive, with the remark that appropriate approaches and methodology are applied to the terms, objectives and circumstances. A research was a combination of quantitative and qualitative research - analyzing the values and the quantity, intensity and practice of enterprises, based on literature analysis and upon her own knowledge, experiences and acquired knowledge, in order to define the concept, construct and hypothesis, further elaboration and data gathering took place through research and survey, data analysis and research results, conclusions and guidelines. Relevant analytical methods have been used, and author's experience in describing and approaching this problem is considered relevant. (Ziemba, 2017)

2.5 Open innovation

"Open innovation in SMEs: Trends, motives and management challenges", by V. van de Vrande, J. P. J. de Jong, W. Vanhaverbeke, M. de Rochemont

The article described Open Innovation phenomenon as innovations' managing approach, a purposeful exchange of knowledge input / output, in order to accelerate internal innovation processes and more successfully emerge on the market by using external innovation through input / output of knowledge, ideas and technology. Authors explored the representation of open innovation practices in small and medium-sized enterprises (SMEs). By analyzing the data of 605 innovative SMEs in the Netherlands, the growth trend of this practice has been established. Open innovations were measured by eight practices applied in SMEs. Research has shown that SMEs in this area have been active over the past 7 years, without significant difference between production and services, and medium-sized enterprises were more represented than small businesses. Motivation for open innovation was mostly tied up with customers and competition tracking. The most important challenges relate to organizational and cultural issues as a result of business with external contacts. (De Vrande et. al, 2009)

The hypothesis could be articulated in the following heading: "The Impact of Open Innovation Practices in Small and Medium Enterprises is related to Adaptation to Market Conditions". The article was focused onto scientific development research, and was based upon the results of surveys, scientific research and practical experience, application and description of new practices. The research upon 605 innovative SMEs was conducted, based on the results, new practices and methodologies for working with innovative SMEs, in the high technology sector were prepared. (De Vrande et. al, 2009)

The article study area is innovation management, with a very good overview of the literature, the paper contains 49 references. The hypothesis is successfully set up as a research problem. The article describes the research methods, was based upon a survey, conducted in 605 medium and small enterprises (SMEs). As a way of collecting data, the survey and data were listed from the SME database in the Netherlands. The new approach is used by innovative companies in the high technology sector, in SMEs are widely used in medium and small businesses. The conclusions of the article were positive, with the fence that other approaches and methodologies were applied in the segment of large and micro enterprises. Authors combined quantitative and qualitative research - analyzing the values and trends, quantities, intensity and potentials of SME's. Data analysis methods used were relevant, and author's experience in describing and approaching this problem is also useful. (De Vrande et. al, 2009)

Data from the EIM database - the Dutch Institute for Business and Political Research, were used in the research. SME sample was selected with telephone polling. Respondents indicated whether their companies had developed innovations (products, processes, organizations, marketing, etc.) over the past 3 years. They were questioned whether they had an innovation strategy for the company in the previous 7 years. The sample has proportionally included SMEs from the service and manufacturing sectors, and micro enterprises (< 10 employees) are excluded due to limited innovation activities.

All respondents (owners, directors, development leaders), were interviewed, totaling 2230, out of which 1206 (54%) confirmed cooperation. A 5% significant difference test was used (p ¼ 0.23 for industry and p ¼ 0.55 for size class). A total of 605 respondents passed the review phase, which corresponds to the final sample rate of 27%. During the 3rd and 4th survey phase, respondents explained the motivation to include various innovation processes as well as obstacles to the introduction of open innovation practices. The research result was a new approach to innovation and the development of methodologies for innovation management, especially related to SME's in the high technology sector. The results point to a number of conclusions about the sectors of the economy, trends, intensity and grades of SMEs. The results presented in the research point to the intensity of open innovation practices observed at the sample level of innovative SMEs, with an overview of the development of this practice in the innovative SMEs in the Netherlands. (De Vrande et. al, 2009)

The T-test was less suitable for predominantly dependent variables, which influenced the distribution, with the Mann-Whitney test, a w2 test of independent t-test samples, with almost identical results, but also a multivariate variance analysis with size classes as control variables. There were fewer differences between production and services. In the involvement of employees and customers, external networking, there are similarities in production and services, production is emphasized by technology, more often, "R & D outsourcing" is used. SMEs in service industries have shown more entrepreneurial and investment preferences (33%). The trend of open innovation in both sectors is consistently positive. Medium-sized companies are more inclined to adopt open innovations. For issues of technology and practice, medium-sized companies have become more ready. (De Vrande et. al, 2009)

The conclusion is that medium-sized companies adopt and apply the practice of open innovation more often than small businesses. Investigating of the open innovation extent with more detail has led to the division of respondents into "clusters", homogeneous in the application and strategy of open innovations and the organization of innovative practices. The analysis was based on eight variables measuring the frequency of application and use of technology, using the "principal component analysis (PCA)" approach to reduce the number of data dimensions used in analytical techniques to reach homogeneous enterprise groups. Differences among clusters were analyzed by non-parametric tests. Analyzing the sectors, 58% of respondents are listed as manufacturing companies, 55% are medium-sized enterprises, which leads to the conclusion that open innovation practices grow as organizations grow, ie enterprises. The research results have shown that SMEs increasingly adopt open innovation. Particular attention is paid to motivation issues and the challenge of open innovation adopting. Among the most important motives for this practice adopting are market-related reasons, market development and meeting customer needs, leading to growth, better results - market and financial, market share growth. These reasons are mainly related to investments (31%), shareholdings in other companies (31%), but also the involvement of customers in innovation processes. In most SMEs, they believe that a wide range of methods is needed to meet customer needs, as competition can overcome them by newer methods and technologies. Various innovation practices have similar motives in the background - entrepreneurship, investment in other companies, inter-organizational networking, customer involvement, innovation practices for complementary product development, integration of new technologies and marketplace monitoring. (De Vrande et. al, 2009)

Employees' inclusion is somewhat different for medium and small businesses, as part of "internal organizational policies", or encouraging the employee motivation and loyalty promotion, unrelated to the goals of innovation. The critical innovations obstacles were investments and shares in other companies, external participation (48%) and rental of R & D outsourcing. Corporate culture is often cited as an obstacle to joint projects by two or more companies (35%), ie share in the same companies (75%), and involvement of external participants and users (48%). There were also issues of delegating responsibility and tasks, but also in communication between organizations. Open innovation as a practice was considered useful in innovation and change as an approach, not just in SME practice, but also as a thematic and methodological basis for sustainability of ICT and society development. The development of methods and practices of innovation management is part of the EU policy (Horizon 2020) and development agenda, but also the market necessity in the context of intense and continuous changes. SMEs' as one of the leaders of social and economic development intensively follows and introduces this practice, and science gains new ground for research. (De Vrande et. al, 2009)

The analysis of the structure, sector and activities points to new conclusions, and in the analysis of motivation and the challenge of adopting open innovations, it provides the basis for further research and scientific projects in this area. The methodology and results, based on relevant research are the firm basis for further analysis and research, pointing to the significance and potential of this area. The literature demonstrates numerous quality references.

2.6 Measuring E-Government Development
"Methodologies for Measuring E-Government Development: The Croatian Case", by Hajdin and Vrček

Contemporary public sector governance opens various questions and development areas, particularly considering ERP implementation. Additional importance was given to the development and network connecting of various platforms for e-services and e-government solutions, as they became a global trend. EU, USA, as well as national governments that are pushing agenda for ERP implementation and further changes that will support society development according to growing number and type of challenges. That represent rising potential for rapid growth and development, and innovation in various related areas. European countries (EU member state and/or other), are investing great resources and support to information society development, with new measurement and comparation methodologies, mostly focused on economical and financial factors, while strategic goals are set by national government. (Hajdin and Vrček, 2010)

This paper focus was on Croatia and differences between methodological approaches to e-services benefits and results measurement, and their coherence for comparison. Authors conducted Croatian public administration and government e-services analysis and their role in e-government development. In order to support the analysis and approve the findings they have studied methodology and considered timeline, as well as state of the art in the few decades overview. E-government initiatives started in late 1990's and have officially started to develop in 2003 with a start of the project "e-Croatia 2007". To accomplish this task internal measurement methodologies have been developed, which relay on EU guidelines and practices. This allows the government and responsible bodies to compare results with similar projects in Europe. Different countries have developed their own methodologies and measuring ways upon accomplishments and progress of set e-government strategies and goals while implementing and developing e-services. (Hajdin and Vrček, 2010)

Authors have considered also a "Global E-Government", as a project conducted by Brookings Institution, focused on economic studies, foreign policy, global economy and development, governance studies and metropolitan policy programs. Global E-Government has collected data from 1,687 national government websites from 198 different countries all over the world. Their methodology was based on evaluation of stated websites by criteria of: "information availability, service delivery and public access". Authors have presented top-ten countries in those reports, including ranking for Croatia (on 45th position in 2007). In the same report Croatia is stated to have 60% of online services covered by websites, from which 100% have publications online, 80% of them have some sort of databases and 20% have privacy policy as well as security policies. From those pages, 0% adopted to W3C disability accessibility standards. This study also presents differences among world regions. In 2006 average score for Eastern Europe was 30%, while in 2007 it was 32%. Focusing back on Croatia, it scored below average in year 2006 with 28%, but made a big leap in next year where the score was above average (35%). This study was conducted on 198 countries from all over the world. Additionally, authors have considered also "UN e-Government survey" that included much more holistic approach. (Hajdin and Vrček, 2010)

The methodology was based on infrastructure development, human capacity, access to knowledge and information. Since governments are viewing their citizens as "customers" this methodology is also more focused on government-to-citizen (G2C) approach, becoming more common in this field. Their questions are focused on "21 citizens' informative and participatory services" which are grouped in 3 categories: "e-information, e-consultation and e-decision-making". UN survey was conducted on 192 countries from all over the world.

Croatian final 47th place was calculated from 3 main categories in UN survey: Web measure index where Croatia had 0.43, infrastructure index with a result of 0.37 and human capital index of 0.9. As stated, Croatian e-government readiness index was 0.57. When considering methodology as a key approach to projects and case studies, authors have also studied Mareva methodology as a method for analysis of impact of various government e-services, based on "return on investment (ROI) calculations for large public projects and comparable approaches in the private sector".

Furthermore, they considered Value Measuring Methodology (VMM), based on defining, capturing and measuring values associated with e-services not accounted in ROI. They also considered rank in 2008 WiBe methodology, based on economic efficiency assessment with particular focus on e-administration elements. WiBe has 3 main areas of impact. First one is "Monetary economic efficiency" which is divided into two subcategories of "Benefits" and "Costs" for a project. Second area is "Extended economic efficiency" which is also divided into two subcategories of "Urgency of the measure" and "Qualitative, strategic importance". Last area is related to "Economic efficiency from an external point of view" and is considered to be an optional part of WiBe methodology. Worth mentioning is that WiBe methodology is used in German Government and administrative bodies. (Hajdin and Vrček, 2010)

As a conclusion, authors have focused onto key methodologies' differences, data collection and analysis related to e-government projects and services. As we have witnessed, that area had dynamic development in the past decade, as many countries have developed and implemented e-government solutions. As there are limits in resources, in order to avoid high costs and time consuming methodologies, there are necessary activities needed to ensure accurate results, respectful to resource constraints and country priorities. Accordingly, authors were focused onto the use of e-service documents and strategies which greatly influence the way e-services have been developed in various countries and set the criteria for their evaluation. Considering their work as a basis for further research, we have to be aware of the fact that "in the future strategic intentions of certain country should be mapped to benchmark indicators. By such approach we would achieve way for collecting the data according to standardized country reports which would take into consideration their e-strategies as well as other local factors while still enabling cross country analysis." (Hajdin and Vrček, 2010)

2.7 E-Government Development
"Interoperability and Government Performance" by Diana Šimić and Slavko Vidović

9th eeeGovDays, 9-10 May 2011, Ljubljana, Slovenia

Authors presented an overview of the Interoperability and Government Performance, as well as set of conditions related to and limiting the establishment and implementation (Budget limitations, taxes growth, public debt, costs reductions, social benefits cutting (education, research, culture, health...). In order to support crisis solution proposals, they proposed smart investments, instead of nondiscriminate cost cutting, aiming for the objectives realization – 3 E's – improvements in Effectiveness, Efficiency, Economy, citizen centricity, transparency, and participation. As a problem area they stressed strategy execution, organizational silos.

When discussing 3E's, they focused onto performance management and business improvements across corporate performance management, government performance budgeting (post II WW), performance management (1990's), public internal financial control (EU since 2000 for the EC and accessing countries). Additionally they accented importance of vision, mission, outcomes and outputs, as well as KPI's, processes, controls, risk assessment and management, ingormation and communication monitoring. (Šimić and Vidović, 2011)

Authors presented USA Strategic Planning and Performance Management, featuring each aspect of the business activity, regulated by USA Government Performance and Results Act (1993).

They provided the EU definition upon the interoperability as "the ability of disparate and diverse organizations to interact towards mutually beneficial and agreed common goals, involving the sharing of information and knowledge between the organizations, through the business processes they support, by means of the exchange of data between their respective ICT systems". Article 2, Decision 922/2009/EC on interoperability solutions for the European public administration (ISA) (Šimić and Vidović, 2011)

Authors provided also a presentation of the interoperability loop through various aspects, such as political context, legal interoperability, process interoperability, semantic interoperability. They proposed the conceptual model for public services through new approach to users by ensuring aggregate public services, orchestration, secure communications management, and data exchange, founded on basic public services that relate to interoperability facilitators, base registries and external services. (Šimić and Vidović, 2011)

When considering various interoperability types and aspects, authors have stressed technological, process and semantic interoperability, and relevant solutions – operational and legal (EIF, SEMIC.EU, as well as need for new tools and strategies, focusing onto USA – Strategy Markup Language (StratML) and Standard Recommended Practice such as ANSI/AIIM 21:2009. (Šimić and Vidović, 2011)

2.8 Maturity Model
"A Maturity Model for Enterprise Interoperability", by Guédria, Chen and Naudet

Authors have conducted study upon interoperability maturity models and concluded that they are covering only some interoperability aspects. Their paper proposed a maturity model for enterprise interoperability which is elaborated on the basis of existing ones. They considered the Enterprise Interoperability Framework under the standardization process, reviewed existing maturity models for interoperability (at the time of the research conducted) and recalled the basic concepts of the Enterprise Interoperability Framework.Their proposal included model analysis and they discussed it to the details, presented methodology and metrics for maturity levels, and finally, presented conclusions and perspectives for future work. Implying interoperability as a value, authors implied establishing an adequate measure of merit to evaluate the degree of interoperability. (Guédria, Chen & Naudet, 2009)

Considering maturity as one of the possible measures, and the evolution stages towards higher degree of interoperability, authors presented systematic work upon the interoperability maturity assessment that may ensure organization insight into their strengths and weaknesses in terms of ability to interoperate with others, and defining priorities to improve interoperability. There are many maturity models, but few of them were developed for interoperability assessment. This paper and research aim was to to propose a Maturity Model for Enterprise Interoperability (MMEI) which deals with all major aspects of interoperability and covers the main concepts of existing interoperability maturity models. (Guédria, Chen & Naudet, 2009)

The Frameworks for Enterprise Interoperability (FEI), were initially elaborated in INTEROP NoE and have passed CEN/ISO standardization process (CEN/ISO 11354), used as a basis to build this MMEI. Previously, survey and comparison studies have been performed to evaluate existing interoperability maturity models: LISI (Levels of Information System Interoperability), OIM (Organizational Interoperability Model), LCIM (Levels of Conceptual Interoperability Model), and EIMM (Enterprise Interoperability Maturity Model), as well as ISO/15504 (SPICE) although it is not dedicated to A Maturity Model for Enterprise Interoperability 217 interoperability assessment. (Guédria, Chen & Naudet, 2009)

The most of interoperability maturity models focus, in most of cases, on one simple facet of interoperability (data, technology, conceptual, Enterprise modeling, etc.). They are complementary rather than contradictory. (Guédria, Chen & Naudet, 2009)

Consequently it is necessary to structure them into a single complete interoperability maturity model to avoid redundancy and ensure consistency. Authors' goal in this paper was to present a preliminary research result on the development of such a Maturity Model for Enterprise Interoperability. Main relevant interoperability maturity models are mapped to the framework to evaluate their coverage. The Framework for Enterprise Interoperability defines 3 basic dimensions as follows:

- levels of the enterprise interoperation content (data, service, process, business)

- obstacles in three categories (conceptual, technological, and organizational)

- ways in which barriers can be removed (integrated, unified, and federated). (Guédria, Chen & Naudet, 2009)

Organization that need to be able to properly interoperate with others, use various different tools such as guidelines or metrics as useful. Evaluating its interoperability potentiality using the MMEI allows the probability it has to support efficient interoperations, as well as to detect precisely the weaknesses that may become sources of interoperability issues. MMEI defines four levels of interoperability maturity, each one describe a certain degree of capability to establish and/or to improve interoperability. (Guédria, Chen & Naudet, 2009)

- Level 0 (Unprepared), the initial level of interoperability maturity, characterized by closed systems, where resources are not meant to be shared with others.

- Level 1 (Defined), the systems are still entirely distinct, some ad hoc interoperations can take place, but the interoperability remains very limited. Some basic IT devices are connectable.

- Level 2 (Aligned), requires that the company is able to make changes in its system in order to adhere to common formats (imposed by a partner).

- Level 3 (Organized), the enterprise is well organized to deal with interoperability challenges. Interoperability capability is extended to heterogeneous systems, and often in a networked context.

- Level 4 (Adapted), the highest level of interoperability maturity (universal). Companies are able to dynamically adjust and accommodate 'on the fly'. (Guédria, Chen & Naudet, 2009)

The maturity was evaluated only from the interoperability viewpoint, can't be applied for other purpose. High level degree of interoperability can't be achieved for free, as it is costly and time consuming, so each enterprise must define its needed interoperability requirements and planned maturity level. It is not recommended to all enterprise to look for the highest interoperability level regardless of their needs. Authors have proposed the development of a maturity model for enterprise interoperability, with 5 levels of maturity and metrics defined and described. A Maturity Model for Enterprise Interoperability concerns (data, service, process, and business) and the three main problem areas (conceptual, technical, and organizational) were usually dealt by separated distinct maturity models. MMEI is also based on the concepts and notions coming from general system theory, considered as relevant to develop a science base for enterprise interoperability. The MMEI is intended to be used in association with OoEI (Ontology of Enterprise Interoperability) to develop a knowledge based system to support enterprise interoperability analysis and diagnostics. (Guédria, Chen & Naudet, 2009)

2.9 Interoperable Architecture

"Architecture of Interoperable Information Systems, An Enterprise Model-Based Approach for Describing and Enacting Collaborative Businesss Processes", by Ziemann J.

Author claims that complex networks describe a wide range of systems in nature and society. Various examples are including the cell, a network of chemical reactions, and the Internet, a network of routers and computers connected by physical links. Following the work on interoperable information systems conducted in European Research Projects in 2010, the Architecture of Interoperable Information Systems (AIOS) was published as a reference for the construction of interoperating systems and model-based enactment of collaborative business processes. (Ziemann, 2010)

The main elements of the AIOS are:

1. A different data types included in interoperable information system, their relationships

2. A different implementing approaches or interoperable information systems adjusting

3. Technical components concept, architecture implementation aimed - design tools and repositories. (Ziemann, 2010)

The AIOS is reference architecture for the interoperable enterprise information systems development. It was described in Ziemann's work [18] and is based on the results of various interoperability research projects, combining concepts, from Service-oriented Architecture, Collaborative Business and Business Process Modelling, as shown in figure 2. (Ziemann, 2010)

Figure 2: Development of collaborative business processes based on three research fields. Source: Ziemann J. Architecture of Interoperable Information Systems. An Enterprise Model-Based Approach for Describing and Enacting Collaborative Businesss Processes, Wirtschaftsinformatik - Theorie und Anwendung (Ziemann, 2010)

The AIOS represents a building model for development of interoperable systems, adjusting and extending their internal information systems systematically. Accordingly, Ziemans findings and studies represent a solid ground for further research and papers upon interoperability and organization architecture that enables further sustainable development and growth. (Ziemann, 2010)

2.10 Sustainable interoperability

Towards a sustainable interoperability in networked enterprise information systems: Trends of knowledge and model-driven technology, On Next Generation Enterprise Information Systems, by Agostinho, C., Ducq, Y., Zacharewicz, G., Sarraipa, J., Lampathaki, F., Poler, R., Jardim-Goncalves R.

Considering Sustainable Interoperability concept, another important paper autor considered for this pilot paper, was „Towards a sustainable interoperability in networked enterprise information systems: Trends of knowledge and model-driven technology", by Agostinho et al. (Agostinho et al., 2016)

The article pointed at the growing importance of networks in developing IO. The concept of Liquid-Sensing Enterprise (LSE) enables manufacturing industry networks with the necessary facilitators of unobtrusive IO and maintaining its IO over the operational lifecycle. The real IO domain of business information client systems expects the need for a new paradigm that can manage the dynamics of the network, facilitating adaptation throughout the company's lifecycle and LSE networks.

Complex Systems Theory provides a set of heuristics that can be applied to support the formalization of the LSE industrial network and its dynamics, demonstrating that it can be enabled and controlled at the same time to maintain the overall level of interoperability stable. Agostinho et al., pointed at the growing importance of networks in developing IO. The concept of Liquid-Sensing Enterprise (LSE) enables manufacturing industry networks with the necessary facilitators of unobtrusive IO and maintaining its IO over the operational lifecycle. The real domain of IO of business information client systems expects the need for a new paradigm that can manage the dynamics of the network, facilitating adaptation throughout the company's lifecycle and LSE networks.

Complex Systems Theory provides a set of heuristics that can be applied to support the formalization of the LSE industrial network and its dynamics, demonstrating that it can be enabled and controlled at the same time to maintain the overall level of interoperability stable. Today there is a technology suitable for the implementation of such systems, capable of realizing the real, digital and virtual worlds of the LSE. However, isolated, this technology can not meet the requirements for a self-sustaining LSE network. The authors proposed a new metaphor of complexity as a framework for modeling and implementing a mechanism to maintain interoperability in such networked environments. They identify the motives for maintaining the interoperability of networked companies with liquid sensors, have complex and customizable systems as a means of modeling and understanding the relationship between enterprise and business information systems in networked environments. Then existing technology such as modeled IO, agent-oriented or service-oriented and knowledge-based architecture is proposed to give a detailed description of the conceptual solution for sustainability of IO. (Agostinho et al., 2016)

Authors pointed ICT contribution to environmental sustainability by resource consumption reducing, social sustainability promoting through equal access to information ensuring, cultural sustainability enhancing, promoting cultural understanding and helping economic growth and sustainability by boosting growth.

3 Literature review

3.1 Interoperability and enterprise architecture development - Zachman's framework

Zachman's Framework of EA - Zachman's framework is defined as the ontology of the enterprise and the fundamental structure for EA that provides a formal and structured way of viewing and defining the enterprise. This ontology is a two-dimensional classification scheme reflecting the intersection between two classifications.

The first are primitive questions: what, how, when, who, where and why. The second is derived from the philosophical concept of reification, transformation of the abstract idea in the instance. Zachman's framework Reformations were: Identification, Definition, Representation, Specification, Configuration, and Instance. There are no fundaments to define the Zachman framework as a methodology, because there is no specific method or process of collecting, managing or using the information it describes. It is rather the ontology, a scheme for the architectural artifacts - project documents, specifications and models, used to take into account those who target the object (the owner and builder of the business) towards a particular problem (data and functionality, for example) is solved. The frame got its name upon John Zachman, who first developed such concept in the eighties in IBM and was updated several times. (Zachman 2008)

The Zachman framework is presented as a framework, named after John Zachman and represented in many ways. The framework is explained as:

- a framework for organizing and analyzing data

- a framework for enterprise architecture

- Classification system or classification scheme

- a matrix, often in the form of a matrix of 6x6

- a two-dimensional model [10] or an analytical model

- a two-dimensional scheme, used to organize detailed business views. (Zachman 2008)

One of the first studies on ICT's contribution to Sustainable Development was a study by Mansell and When, focusing on leading trends in ICT application in providing state service delivery, productivity, improvement quality of life, alleviating poverty, increasing access to information and disseminating information and facilitating the exchange of knowledge.

The key contribution to the SIS studies was made by Fuchs, coining the term SIS. He defined the SIS share uses ICT to "encourage good life for all human beings present and future generations by strengthening biological diversity, technological usability, economic wealth for all, political participation of all and cultural wisdom". He believes that SIS research should focus on a holistic approach, including environmental, technological, economic, political and cultural issues.

Hilty and Aebischer tried to answer a question of improving the ICT contribution to sustainability. "The transformational power of ICT can be used to sustain our production and consumption patterns, but technology history has shown that increased energy efficiency does not contribute to automatic sustainability. ICT for Creating a Sustainable Society ICT's potential for SIS development can be derived from two aspects: as an industry and as a tool. (Hilty and Aebischer, 2014)

Nikpay et al. in "A hybrid method for evaluating enterprise architecture implementation", proposed a model of evaluation upon an EA implementation theory. They proposed an EA in-depth study, artefacts, and EA Body of Knowledge (EABK), the evaluation extension through the provision of information on evaluation practice, identification of EA assessment challenges, provision of relevant knowledge of the necessary development practices EA estimates. Evaluation of EA implementation provides a set of methods and practices for assessing EA performance artifacts within the EA implementation project. Existing practices in models of EA function and process estimation are using structured methods in developing EA implementation, maturity analysis and measures to achieve the appropriate assessment. The aim of the research was to develop a hybrid evaluation method that supports the achievement of the EA implementation goals. The proposed method was developed on the basis of literature review, semi-structured interviews with EA practitioners, assessment of program theory, and assessment of information systems. The proposed method was confirmed by case studies and expertise. Research provides a basis for researchers who want to expand knowledge and continue with this research topic by further analysis and research. (Nikpay et al. 2017)

Hinkelmann et al. in "A new paradigm for the continuous alignment of business and IT" prosposed a paradigm for IS meeting needs of a new enterprise generation for continuous business alignment and ICT for agile business. They argued whether metamodeling supports human-interpreted business architecture models and constructive ontology of enterprises that can be interpreted, as well as semantic raise transforms metamodels for business architecture into constructive enterprise ontology, as semantic metamodels express the semantics of modeling concepts by ontology. Examples of new generation business information systems are presented including modeling tools and model analysis algorithms, identification of need for adaptation and risk assessment. The paper deals with information systems for new generations in the context of business engineering. (Hinkelmann et al. 2016)

They propose a new paradigm for next generation enterprise information systems for the continuous alignment of business and IT for the agile enterprise. The metamodelling approach supports human-interpretable EA models and machine-interpretable enterprise ontologies. Semantic lifting transforms metamodels for the EA into machine-interpretable enterprise ontologies. Semantic metamodels express the semantics of all modelling concepts by an ontology. The ontology is extended by a metamodel, which defines the notation and syntax of the graphical modelling language. Examples of next generation enterprise information systems are described, and embedded modelling tools and algorithms for model analysis, identification of adaptation needs, and risk assessment. The paper deals with Next Generation Enterprise Information Systems in the context of Enterprise Engineering. The continuous alignment of business and IT in a rapidly changing environment is a grand challenge for today's enterprises. The ability to react timeously to continuous and unexpected change is called agility and is an essential quality of the modern enterprise. Being agile has consequences for the engineering of enterprises and enterprise information systems. In this paper a new paradigm for next generation enterprise information systems is proposed, which shifts the development approach of model-driven engineering to continuous alignment of business and IT for the agile enterprise. It is based on a metamodelling approach, which supports both human-interpretable graphical enterprise architecture and machine-interpretable enterprise ontologies. Furthermore, next generation enterprise information systems are described, which embed modelling tools and algorithms for model analysis. (Hinkelmann et al. 2016)

Bakar et al. presented the evaluation of EA and public-sector implementation opportunities in the "Assessment of Enterprise Architecture Implementation Capability and Priority in Public Sector Agencies". The purpose of the study was to evaluate the ability and priorities of the EA implementation in the Malaysian public sector agency. Study uses the Analytical Hierarchy Process (AHP), based on judgments and opinions of EA team members from three different federal agencies.

Bin Wu et al. in "Configuration and Operation Architecture for a Dynamic Cellular Manufacturing Product Service System" described the sustainability of architecture and IO. Sustainability and reconfiguration of the Dynamic Cellular Product System (DCMS) plays a significant role for companies in preparing a fast response to the market that is changing and increasing their competitive power. Due to the lack of effective standards for the implementation of manufacturing and service integration, the problem remains the architecture of the Configuration and Operation Operations for the DCMS supporting the Production Service System (PSS). In order to improve the sustainability and reconfiguration of DCMS, the Dynamic Cellular Manufacturing Product Service (DCM-PSS) configuration and operating architecture is presented, based on the function block and the key configuration and operation techniques DCM-PSS has been studying. (Bin Wu et al. 2016)

Tao Zhi-Gang et al. in the "Enterprise application architecture development based on DoDAF and TOGAF" study, support design and analysis of enterprise application architecture, point to a custom framework for describing enterprise application architecture and appropriate design methods. The framework shown can effectively support services-oriented architecture and cloud computing by creating metadata based on architectural content (ACF), DoDAF metamodel (DM2), and CCMN (Cloud Computing Modeling Notation). The framework also seeks to expand and improve mapping between Architectural Inputs / Exits of Open Architecture Architecture (TOGAF), delivered products and models described within Architecture of the Department of Defense Architecture (DoDAF). The 52 model outlined in DoDAF is constructed by generating the metamodels of these described models and by analyzing the limited relationship between the metamodels. (Tao Zhi-Gang et al. 2015)

Olsen and Trelsgård in the "Enterprise Architecture Adoption Challenges: An Exploratory Case Study of Norwegian Higher Education" illustrate the challenges of EA implementation and solutions in the Norwegian higher education sector. Contemporary business architecture is a challenge for the implementation of Enterprise Architecture (EA) in the organization. This is also the case in the public sector, such as public universities and faculties. (Olsen and Trelsgård 2016)

There is a very limited research on such issues. It is therefore important to explore how EA is implemented in different sectors, which benefits are achieved and which challenges are most prominent. This interpretative case study explores EA joint efforts in the Norwegian higher education sector. The authors argue that progress was hampered by the lack of the highest levels of administration by the ministry, the lack of a comprehensive architecture council, and the lack of EA expertise at the highest level of governance in individual institutions. The most noteworthy advantages are business agility, economies of scale, and better decision making. (Olsen and Trelsgård 2016)

Edvinsson and Aderinne in "Enterprise Architecture Made Simple: Using the Ready, Set, Go Approach to Achieving Information Centricity" pointed to the EA implementation growth and diverse capabilities, described how to start fast and establish a basic line for EA within ten weeks, then grow and stabilize the architecture over time using proven access (Ready, Set, Go, Ready, Go). They provided instructions on how to set up and implement EA and point out a possibility to build close relationships with stakeholders and delivery teams. EA has to provide space for both current and unknown business initiatives, and it is also necessary to get a holistic view of the EA implementation process. Everyone must be aware that information is a key business resource and that information architecture is a key part of the company's architecture. The Ready-Set-Go method for introducing enterprise architecture provides an understanding of the basic steps for starting, organizing, and managing your organization's overall architecture. (Edvinsson and Aderinne 2013)

Nan Niu et al. presented information organization systems and their analysis and evaluation in the work of Enterprise Information Systems Architecture-Analysis and Evaluation. Numerous SW design proposals are available to ICT engineers in developing their business information systems. Although these suggestions and methodologies help engineers in designing architecture, the systematic methods for evaluating SW architecture are scarce. In order to appropriately choose the appropriate SW architecture between different options, a scenario-based approach was suggested to assess how SW architecture affects the fulfillment of business requirements. The empirical assessment of the SW supply chain selection has shown that the developed approach provides extraordinary insight into SW development and can be included in the practice of moderate cost ICT systems. (Nan Niu et al. 2013)

Lapalme et al., in "Exploring the Future of Enterprise Architecture: A Zachman Perspective", gave an overview of EA development from the "Zachman" perspective. Zachman's framework is used to identify and consider future major EA challenges. Models and theories that could be useful in dealing with identified major challenges for EA were considered. There has been progress in the field of EA application. Research evolution development futuristic scenarios, education and business architecture of companies were presented. Today and in the foreseeable future, organizations will face increasing levels of complexity and uncertainty. EA should help facing the toughest design of adaptive and resilient businesses and their information systems. The paper presents the "Great Challenges" that we think will cause challenges to organizations in the future and should be addressed by EA. (Lapalme et al. 2015)

Nishimura et al. provided precise view of IO in virtual organizations in the work "Virtual organization platform interoperability provides the long tail and eScience environment". The core eScience technology is to connect distributed resources as a virtual instance, enabling collaborative research for shared virtualized resource. The eScience first accepted common resources through support of "great science" in the Grid Computing. New cloud services create superior eScience infrastructure such as shared computer and disk resources available to joint researchers. Users must always be certified as researchers and licensed when they use services that provide specific co-operation. Effective exploitation of the global implementation of academic alliances can enable us to build a more coherent and coherent eScience environment more secure, simpler and more scalable. One of the most significant recent trends in the Federation of Identities is support for a virtual organization (VO), an organization that consists of individuals who are mostly domiciled and authenticated against the organization but act in a certain role within a virtual organization. (Nishimura et al. 2016)

D'Elia et al. in "Enabling Interoperability in the Internet of Things: A OSGi Semantic Information Broker Implementation" show the growing importance of Internet technology as a link to Interoperability between different formats, protocols and platforms. This allows the connection and vision of heterogeneous devices and services on IoT. Semantic web technologies can be applied to a wide range of contexts of application (automation, industry, health care, defense, finance, smart cities, etc.) involving heterogeneous actors (users, communities, public authorities, businesses). Smart-M3 is a semantic publishing and subscription architecture designed to connect a semantic web and an Internet domain. It is based on the SGB (Semantic Information Broker) where data is stored as RDF graphs and software agents using SPARQL to update, download, and subscribe to changes in the data repository. This article describes the implementation of OSG SIB with the new persistent SPARQL update. The OSGi SIB performance is evaluated and compared with the reference implementation C. Finally, the first upload on Android is displayed. (D'Elia et al. 2017)

Doumeingts and Chen in "European Initiatives to Develop Interoperability of Enterprise Applications – Basic Concepts, Framework and Roadmap" presented EU initiatives to concept development, framework and guidelines for IO development. Their work presents basic concepts, frameworks and guidelines for developing IO of business applications and software. It is a summary of the main work done in the EU to develop IO development plans and prepare the forthcoming research and development projects under the Sixth Framework Program (FP6). The authenticity of the approach is solving IO problems from multiple but integrated views. Contemporary user requirements and vision for interoperability development, as well as recommendations for future work were presented. (Doumeingts and Chen 2003)

Green et al. in "Ontological Evaluation of Enterprise Systems Interoperability Using ebXML" gave an overview of the IO system developed among organizations. Enterprise Systems Interoperability (ESI) becomes the current business theme. This is manifested by the number and scope of proxy candidates for process IO, ie EbXML, BPML, BPEL, and WSCI. Along with the wide support for each of these candidate standards, despite broad acceptance, no sound theoretical assessment of these approaches has yet been provided. Authors use the Bunge-Wand-Weber (BWW) model as a representation model to provide a basis for theoretical assessment. They pointed to the utility of the national representation model for analysis, evaluation and engineering in the area of traditional and structured system analysis, object oriented modeling and modeling processes. (Green et al. 2005)

This paper deals with the question of potential semantic weaknesses in the use of ebXML for the process of interoperability between business systems? They found that users lacked important implementation information due to representative disadvantages; due to ontological redundancy, unnecessarily increased complexity of the specification; the user of the specification will have to bring an external model of knowledge and understand the constructs in the specification due to the cases of ontological surplus. (Green et al. 2005)

Panetto et al. in "Ontological approach for products-centric information system IO in networked manufacturing enterprises" are at odds with the growing importance of standardization in the development and application of IO. Standardization Initiatives (ISO and IEC) are trying to respond to the heterogeneous information management problems scattered within organizations by formalizing knowledge about product technical information. Although the product is a central facility from which, throughout its life cycle, all business systems are within a single enterprise or between collaborative networked companies, they have a specific view, we can consider it active if it participates in the decisions it brings by providing knowledge about oneself. This paper proposes a new approach, assuming that the product, which is the technical data, can be considered interoperable by itself with many applications that concern manufacturing companies if they incorporate knowledge about themselves, because they store all their technical data, provided they are built into a common model . The issue of this approach is the formalization of all technical data and concepts that contribute to the definition of product ontology, embedded in the product itself and making it interoperable with applications, reducing the loss of semantics. (Panetto et al. 2009)

Vernadat in "Technical, Semantic and Organizational Issues of Enterprise Interoperability and Networking" provides an overview of business framework development as well as business integration and interoperability. Networking organizations refer to all kinds of structures in which two or more geographically dispersed business entities need to interact. This can happen within a networked enterprise or between several companies, including an expanded enterprise or a virtual organization. This refers to any kind of organization, eg industrial companies, public organizations or large government agencies. Enterprise interoperability is a sine qua-condition for enterprise integration and networking. It mainly relies on information and communication technology (ICT), especially on Internet computing. The paper uses the European Framework for Interoperability (EIF) as the basis for the first discussion on technical, semantic and organizational aspects of interoperability and networking, and finally addressing some of the open research questions. (Vernadat, 2009)

Cretan et al. in "NEGOSEIO: A Framework for Negotiating Sustainable Enterprise Interoperability" point to new challenges of IO and sustainability. The development of the Internet and competitiveness encourage companies to develop better solutions with less resources, follow new trends and support new platforms and methodologies. Legislation and regulations are updated frequently and deeply, and require rapid corporate compliance. These frequent business changes shake off all IO links between companies, leading to a period of adjustment where business is not possible. (Cretan et al. 2012)

This paper suggests that the best way for a strong IO environment is to carry out continuous, periodic maintenance operations to help companies adapt to the environmental ecosystem. NEGOSEIO as a framework promotes continuous improvement and adaptation of business interoperability management and negotiation as a key mechanism for addressing inconsistencies and solutions to identified interoperability problems. Following this approach, businesses will adapt to changes and external factors, and thus develop elastic and effective supply chain interactions. This work confirms the framework by applying in the real business case of designing an aviation mission to the European Space Agency (ESA). (Cretan et al. 2012)

4 The I3O concept – contribution to further public administration and social development

I3O support public administration and its development functionalities. The paper thesis is that *sustainable I3O systems are ensuring the SIS development and vice versa*, interacting with IO, and contributing to SIS. Following to the thesis, author planned to conduct a research in order to contribute to a metamodel development and presentation of interdependence of organization development, particularly for the integration into SITS. There is also a need to present the types and levels of IO as a part of SIO development, so it is necessary to conduct the survey with questionnaires, that will ensure the data, for the further analysis, and to test the hypothesis. This work focuses on the I3O, particularly the public administration I3O, closely related to research planned for the future PhD dissertation. The work consists of the following components:

- a literature overview related to I3O and SIO as a concept,

- the concept of SIO as a critical point of future SITS development,

- a description of set of communication and coordination activities,

- theoretical model and a construct development for future processes description,

- the methodology and the presentation of future studies as a platform for future research.

4.1 Research on I3O concept and its contribution to SIS develoment

I3O concept is planned to be developed upon the research and an adequate evaluation regarding its relation to previously mentioned components, concepts and information. In order to ensure the concept development, contemporary organisations are evaluating their work to check they meet their intended outcomes and to improve their practice. Author considered components that need to be ensured for I3O concept effects and efficiency (Figure 3):

- standardization,
- communication,
- harmonization,
- coordination,
- implementation
- conceptualization.

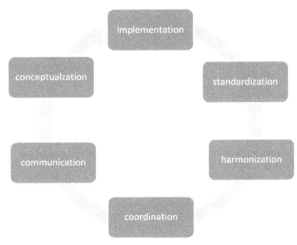

Figure 3: I3O components for concept effects and efficiency

An evaluation of the values and activities may lead to following assumptions:

- project impacts on the existing and future status, methodology - way how to reach the goal
- open-ended research opening a space and encountering the unexpected or negative findings
- focus and measure of things that author consider significant
- focus onto particular area, as research has to detect contextual information.

5 New technologies and potentials

The potential for BCT applications for governments, public administration and large embedded systems has not yet been systematically researched, although there is growing number of publications in the field of ICT application in industry, public administration, large and complex systems. Most of those papers upon the BCT often points out opportunities and technological advantages, but omits pointing out BCT challenges, such as deployment, concealed constraints, materiality and management issues that can limit these potentials. There are growing expectations regarding various interpretations of concepts, environments and trends, presenting the concept of BCT, literature, about the possible benefits of applying this technology, which became the subject of increasing number of debates in science, business and the general public. Critical review of the concept of BCT is an indispensable part of the analysis as a basis for conclusions and guidelines. This point leads to the existence or absence of the concept of research, as a subject of research. (Janssen et al., 2017)

On October 31, 2008, a special manifestation "Bitcoin - Electronic Cash System" was published by the mysterious Satoshi Nakamoto. The described Bitcoin system was launched as a digital service on January 3, 2009. In the period of 2009, the digital currency system has gone up all the expectations and the cryptovalue of Bitcoin in the market has jumped dozens of thousand times with uninvited announcements and projections up to $ 100,000, and total turnover in excess of $ 60 billion in the mid 2017. Currently, the most known BC application in the world of finance, but with even more important implications, leads to the establishment of an ecosystem of innovative ideas and services extending beyond the financial sector. (Janssen et al., 2017)

5.1 Blockchain tehnologies

Although the original BC application Bitcoin was primarily focused on crypto currency transactions, since its inception in 2009, the development of BCT has expanded the range of sectors beyond the financial domain. Applications range from simple transactions and information exchange to complex processes, and sophisticated contracts can be used to regulate these transactions. The public sector has a range of services and transactions that would make use of the BCT's benefits and these potentials should certainly be appropriately explored with a view to understanding potential benefits in order to better identify areas of effective use in public administration. (Janssen et al., 2017)

In the study of interoperability, information systems and the development of a sustainable information society, there is an increasing emphasis on conceptual understanding, so it is particularly important to define the conceptual framework that should contribute, as a framework to study interoperability, with the possibility of further adaptation. Bitcoin was the first system with BC data structure and the basis for all BCT implementations in a wide range of domains, such as energy, music industry and healthcare. BCT is also known as DLT (Distributed Ledger Technology), and is based on the idea that each participant has access to a shared book (base or "ledger"). The idea of an open access, universally accessible book was born with Bitcoin, and the system provided the first solution to the problem of trust building in an uncertain environment without reliance on third parties. (Janssen et al., 2017)

There is a well-known challenge, known as the Byzantine Generals problem, which concerns the army of generals where every general commands part of the army and are located in different places. Generals have different preferences and locations, some nodes can "play" to communicate on behalf of the general, and together they must make decisions about whether they are attacking, withdrawing, or taking any other actions. In the Byzantine failure knot (representing the general) can be pretended to be accurate, but it presents different responses to different nodes for manipulating outcomes. In digital currency research this problem is solved by using the Nakamoto Consensus to avoid double consumption. (Janssen et al., 2017)

The basic idea of the BCT is to enable digital asset transaction nodes using a P2P network that stores those transactions over a distributed network. Property owners and transactions involving ownership change are entered in the book by using cryptography of public keys and digital signatures. Each transaction confirms nodes in the network using a "consensus mechanism". This works in such a way that at each transaction entry in the P2P network, the nodes first confirm the transaction. If the nodes confirm legitimacy, they confirm the transaction, and this decision is determined by the block. The new block is added to the previous chain of blocks and thus becomes locked. The latest block maintains a common, agreed opinion on the current state of BC. To illustrate how the BCT works, we use the so-called "Smart contract". BCT can be used to develop smart contracts storing a deal on the participant terms and when the conditions are met, the changes in the contract will be made. A smart contract defines the rules and penalties around the agreement and automatically executes and enforces the contractual obligation. A smart deal can be defined as "a mechanism involving digital assets and two or more parties where some or all of the parties place assets and assets are automatically redistributed among these parties according to the formula based on certain information that is not known at the time of the beginning of the contract. a program that runs in BC and has its proper execution by implementing a consensus protocol, contains agreement information and will only be executed if the conditions are validated by all nodes in the network. (Janssen et al., 2017)

A simple example to illustrate such a contract is the transfer of property ownership. The buyer of the house invests the amount of money to pay for the property. Only if the buyer submits his key to the seller within a certain time, the payment is processed and the asset is updated in BC. If the key is not transferred, the money is returned to the buyer. The contract contains the rules of the transaction that can not be changed during the process, neither of the parties would interfere with it, unless someone else knows it, and may explain how the parties have to confirm the transfer before the contract is executed to avoid the dispute and secure the trust. Another example of application of the BCT may be voting in the elections. A "Smart contract" can provide one-time voting and proper ballot verification, reducing the possibility of voter fraud and manipulation of results due to a distributed node network and a distributed consensus protocol that ensures the integrity of voice data being broadcast. The use of these mechanisms can automate part of the mediating role of notary public in the sale of real estate, although the BCT can not automatically automate important notarial roles such as drafting contracts and checking compliance and contract execution. In order to fully understand the potential of these clever contracts, and to avoid mistakes, further research is needed. (Janssen et al., 2017)

The key difference between BCT and conventional digital technologies derives from distributed P2P nature. BCs consist of distributed books that are synchronized via P2P mechanisms and pre-agreed rules about which new data can be added. This deviates from conventional situations where one party maintains a database with all data and decides on the responsibility for creating, reading, updating and deleting (CRUD) data. Data management by one organization is less complex as responsibilities can be centrally coordinated, although it is challenging in practice. Such a centralized architecture is in contrast to BCT, where every node on the network has a full copy of the transaction. BCT is a significant contribution to data integrity compared to current implementations, meaning that the data stored in the system matches the actual view. Data Integrity refers to a wide range of aspects such as consistency, security, reliability, timeliness, non-viability and non-manipulation that need to be guaranteed. The BC distribution ensures that manipulating and modifying data without consensus becomes more and more difficult, resulting in better information integrity, though complete integrity can never be guaranteed. (Janssen et al., 2017)

6 Applying new technologies and potential issues
BCT is an innovative technology that offers new ways of organizing and accessing a number of areas for registering transactions, events, processes, and records. It is about the form of distributed bases in which transactions are democratized by introducing consensus mechanisms that enable the transaction. While BCT applications in the private sector are ever increasing, BCT offers a number of potential benefits in the area of e-government.

Those benefits are not easy to accomplish because of the system size and complexity, as well as implications for public administration that should be explored through a series of research - strategic, organizational, economic, information and technological aspects. There are still doubts that achieving such advantages could be more difficult than the idea itself. Janssen et al.discussed two perspectives for governments regarding the growth in application of BCT and its related applications. On the one hand, a perspective in which public organizations adopt BCT for providing services in which BCT uses to manage transactions. The second perspective is called BC Governance, which determines how the BC should look, adjust itself to change, and ensure fulfillment of public values and social needs. Both require deep knowledge of the BCT and the current situation. A special challenge is the immaturity of the BCT itself, which is still in development. For deployment of large-scale BCTs, it's important to design flexibility, one of the most important design criteria for e-government systems. This requires precise and decisive management, the BCT's future features have embedded mechanisms (consensus and file-changer protocol), which are inconsistent with flexibility. Critical assessment uses BC for e-government requires research on changes in data management and government roles responsibility. (Janssen et al., 2017)

Additional studies and research are needed in order to ensure confidence creating, mediation, organizational transformation, management models, design variables, auditing, and effects on the benefits and limitations. This requires developing the process between technology still in development and finding responses appropriately managed in order to stimulate the positive effects of using environmental applications while at the same time mitigating any unwanted consequences for society as a whole. The process of experimenting governments themselves for BCT applications in their own services seems to be the most important in order to gain a deeper understanding of BCT work as a complex socio-technical system and to find and possibly redefine its own roles and functions in a changing institutional environment. (Janssen et al., 2017)

BCT can be used for any transaction or exchange of information in which the government is involved. Basic features of BCT enable deployment in the range of asset inventory, inventory and information exchange, physical assets and intangible assets such as votes, patents, ideas, reputation, intent, health data, etc. It means that organizations can keep track of the book and jointly create, evolve and keep track of the invariable transaction history and determine successive events. Governments from around the world are piloting BCTs. Entries in BCT are of a different nature and include digital identity, storage of court decisions, eg funding of school buildings and fund and fund raising, marital status, e-voting, business licenses, passports, criminal records and tax records.

Authors recommend further research to analyze the source of benefits and transaction situations. A good example is the events and gatherings organization that depends on the municipality, police, fire brigade and healthcare organizations and insurance. As another example we can also take car ownership. In an attempt to find the owner, the car transaction history must be analyzed, assuming it contains a unambiguous property identifier. The owner is identified by searching the book because everyone has the same look at BC. The rule says that only the owner can sell a car. When a car is sold, a transaction should be created in which the previous owner confirmed the sale of the car, the new owner confirms the purchase of the car, and the bank confirms the transfer for ownership transfer. Another example is an overview of authority in public administration and the ability to change only if there is an agreement between nodes classified as ranked higher in the hierarchy. Each node in the network contains a full copy of BC, transactions are recorded in the database, and each node has access to a full transaction history. Access to the main book may be limited, and it is necessary to determine the number of nodes as well as the type of consensus mechanism. The final example of using BCT is landscaping projects.

BCT is useful when proprietary records are not kept in a systematic manner or if a business organization is not trusted. In some countries, it is difficult to disclose land ownership. In addition to the BCT application, each transaction of land value must be registered, which prevents manipulation and loss of data. The transfer of land property requires that the lawful owner must sign, for which proof of ownership should be, no mortgage should be on the real estate, and the transfer of money from the purchase on the sales side must be secured. However, BCT does not help with the accuracy of ownership, but tries to clarify authenticity. In case the input manipulates and meets the conditions, the network will accept it and add it to BC. BC can be used as one of the tools to combat land registry corruption, but it should be part of a wider institutional framework, including other instruments for legal certainty and land registry compliance. (Janssen et al., 2017)

7 Proposed research and study of the future concept for potential application

7.1 Development of the I3O Concept - Background and Motivation of Research

As one of the key components of organization and public administration, interoperability ensures the functioning of communication and the development of entrepreneurship. With more than 10 years of experience in public administration work, especially with EU-related activities, with experience in working in major global companies, the author has dedicated his career to studies related to organization, business development, information technology, communications and related areas. He confirmed his interest in the organization and development of the company, interrelated, focusing on the study of organization and development of ICT. The author considered his experiences in large organizations, public administration and large private companies, supporting the development of ICT, implementation and adoption, as well as interoperability leading to the sustainable development of the information society.

New ICTs are insufficiently explored, interoperability and development are described in a variety of academic and business publications. However, there is an increasing need for a concept that will contribute to sustainable interoperability and the development of the information society. I3O as a concept recognizes interoperability problems in large systems, businesses and public administration in general, various issues and areas of improvement as well as the need for continuous development and open architecture involving new elements and restructuring.

The impact of interoperability on synergies and system development, as well as on further concepts, implications and consequences, is not sufficiently developed or explored to contribute to the new paradigm for an increasing number of systems and networks involved. To support the concept, the author plans to conduct research on the development of the I3O concept. Public administration, following the development of society, the development of ICT and its influence on society at all support the adoption of ICT, implementation and contribution to further development of SIS through various fields: e-government, e-citizens, state support programs new educational programs, having in mind mutual influence and support for sustainable social development.

This paper aims to support the development of the I3O concept, research and description, as well as contribution to development and implementation. Research I3O has the following goals:

1) Building a framework for the development and implementation of the concept I3O,

2) Contribution to future research of the I3O concept,

3) Linking the I3O concept to the application of new technologies.

In developing and testing the I3O concept, the author considers significant individual experiences, relevant literature and research in the given field. Based on personal experiences, the author has found the development of interoperability and his contribution to the development of a further viable information society of immense importance and motivating for research. Bearing in mind the need for a concept that will ensure the development of interoperability, within public administration, adopting a new paradigm, stimulating innovation and proactive policies, in a new environment, the author considers the significant articulation of such concept and its further development as the basis for and possible guidance for a possible future research on public administration architecture and the application of new ICT. The increase in the number of scientific papers in this area has led the author to consider the sources of the application of new ICTs in public administration and further development in the conditions of more pronounced, more complex and bigger changes.

The author considered his own personal and professional experience relevant to the initiative and support of this and similar concepts, literature and modern business and science that led to the conclusion that there is an increasing need for I3O. Considered the strengths, weaknesses, opportunities and threats (SWOT analysis), and identified the need for intuitive and conceptual systems to provide a way for adaptation of new technologies and sustainable development of the information society. The strengths of the system are in a large number of qualified, employed educated experts, their networking, networking and involvement, financial and political power that enable and support policy implementation, their capabilities are their ability and influence on virtually all processes in the contemporary society, the potential for negotiation, the absorption and development of new ICT, organizational and scientific projects and solutions, and thus the ability to influence the market, the economy, society in general.

There are also threats due to the complexity and lack of flexibility, adaptability and standards at certain organizational levels, economically and politically. Emphasizing weaknesses, such as excessive complexity, growth and development, it is difficult to plan, organize, integrate and develop systems and individual subsystems and elements, and the need for specific solutions to grow. These solutions need a multidisciplinary approach and an open architecture for further development and adaptation to new environmental changes. In order to construct such a concept that will encompass different approaches, integration and maintenance of a flexible platform for further development, the author has considered a possible solution to the concept of inter-institutional interoperability (I3O). When discussing the challenges that led to this idea, the author was primarily focused on organizational issues and abilities, adaptability, and the disadvantages of organizational culture that supports organizational change and improvement through the development of interoperability. He has conducted several case studies, reviewing literature and topics, relevant to this and some future research. To explore these concepts, it is necessary to ensure an adequate approach, because here political power plays a key role in setting goals, transformation into policies and strategies, programs and projects, leading to outcomes that are not always adequately and logically endorsed by arguments.

There is a strong need to consider research on how the initiatives and activities of interoperability depend on political and cultural issues in organizations, so it needs to support changes in the development and incorporation of the I3O concept and bring it into line with cultural changes.

7.2 Research Objectives

The research objectives include the following:

• An overview of the relationship between development of interoperability and public administration development through the development and application of the I3O concept,

• The relationship between interoperability and modern public administration is extremely important and must be determined,

• Monitoring changes in interoperability through possible research and progress,

• Identification of key factors, targeted results and outcomes.

7.3 Research research question and hypothesis

The research question and hypothesis reads - can interoperability contribute to the development of organization and public administration system in a sustainable and efficient way? The field of research is information science. We do not know in advance the answer. An example of the hypothesis of the research may be: Due to the rules and standards of interoperability it is impossible to develop 100% reliable systems that operate under unpredictable conditions. The thesis should include interoperability, variables and standards, patterns, corporate culture, adoption of ICT, architecture and links with other relevant issues. The author plans to combine primary and secondary data and contribute to the development of the paradigm as well as the basis for further research on this subject. Data from books, studios, journals, online or offline, are part of the studies and play an important role in the reliability of research, given a number of criteria that are not limited to the release date, authors credibility, source reliability, quality of hearing, depth of analysis , the scope of the text contribution to the development of the research area

When considering primary data collection, the collection of quantitative data is based on mathematical calculations in various forms, including questionnaires on participant issues in related processes and activities, correlation and regression methods, middle, mode, and media, and others. While concluding quantitative methods, the author has provided space for inclusion of qualitative research methods, does not include numbers or mathematical calculations associated with words, sounds, emotions, colors, and other quantizable elements. Accordingly, in order to ensure a greater level of depth of understanding, the author will include interviews, open questionnaires, focus groups, observation, play or role play, case studies, etc. for quality data collection methods

7.4 Methods of analysis of data

The methodology for this research will include discussions on data analysis methods to explain how primary data will be analyzed and applied by methods. According to the difference between qualitative and quantitative data analysis, qualitative researches using interviews, case studies, experiments and so on. The data analysis will include identifying patterns within the response and critically analyzing them in order to achieve the research goals. On the other hand, the analysis of data for the quantitative part will include critical analysis and interpretation of the results. Primary research results comparation with the literature review results are important.

Concepts IO and I3O support public administration and development - The goal is that sustainable I3O systems ensure the development of a sustainable information society and vice versa, in interaction with IO. The author plans to conduct research to contribute to the development of metamodel and to present the interdependence of the organization's development. There is also a need to show types and levels of IO, so it is advisable to conduct questionnaire surveys, for further analysis and hypothesis testing. This paper focuses on I3O and public administration, closely related to research planned for future doctoral dissertation. The work will include the following:

- review and analysis of I3O literature as a concept,

- presentation and interpretation of concept I3O as a new contribution to the development of public administration,

- a theoretical model and developmental structure for the description of future processes,

- methodology and presentation of future studies as a platform for future research.

The I3O concept is designed to develop on the basis of research and assessment related to the connection to the concepts mentioned above. To ensure the development of the concept, modern organizations evaluate their work to see if they meet the intended goals and improve their practice. The author considered the components to be provided for the expected I3O results:

- standardization,

- communication,

- harmonization,

- coordination,

- implementation

- conceptualization.

The purpose of this paper is to provide a platform for I3O concept research, including quality and efficiency, and support and enhancement of collaboration within a networked environment. To achieve a certain level of IO, researchers collect data, determine IO levels, and goals. The further development of such trends and the re-use of results is a critical challenge for researchers, existing, future and previous research teams. Sustainable development of the interoperability system is linked to and complemented by IT systems and networks that have built-in interoperability and continuously ensure development and sustainability with all aspects of architecture, organization, products, services, culture, etc.

Contemporary business, technology and science, as well as public administration, are mostly dependent on ICT support and contribution, a variety of networks and systems based on ICT, as well as new and developed systems leading to new ICT and post-information society.

In order to ensure sustainable adaptation, support and implementation of various systems and ICTs in general, serious efforts are being made to build higher levels of knowledge and recognition of human-level interoperability as human point of view is a key factor. The human factor is linked to decisions and interoperability depends on it.

7.5 Building a Sustainable Interoperability System

Recent studies and technological development ensure technical issues are important. Taking into account the problems of IO, EA, system development and maintenance of points, we are mainly focused on technical issues with regard to measurable values, definitions, standards, etc. Analyzing from a human point of view, we are facing problems with the machine compatibility point. Artificial intelligence meets human operational standards and mimics human operations. Contemporary companies combine services, seeking balance between critical points - both human and technical. Building a sustainable system, interoperable and standardized, needs a critical ingredient - people. Regardless of the fact that people can replace many technical points and roles, there are certain things people still keep for them - make decisions. Decisions are a key point for IO, communication and further development. The public administration faces difficult choices due to the size and complexity of the ICT influence, with the additional need for IO, as services move towards the concept of smart systems.

Researchers should consider open innovations that provide functionality and platform for further development of services. Recent studies on "smart cities" and "sustainable architecture" have shown the need for ICT, especially the Internet. The Republic of Croatia faces various challenges for the standardization, development and implementation of ICT in public administration. By building a platform to address complex issues, researchers need to consider different impacts to define measures that will ensure a higher level of standardization, alignment and integration, ensuring a higher level of IO. The construction of such a system is based on an analysis of existing potential, possible growth and improvement. There is a strong need to define influences that affect IO, such as political, economic, and social. Measuring these values depends on the basic components. When considering standardization and integration capabilities, measurable values (ISO defined or other standard processes are a good example) need to be considered.

Regardless of forecasts and development potential, public services still need additional support in achieving higher levels of IO, as they continue to expect results in organizational development and IO level. Technical support and development require convergence, and further development depends on their harmonization. The paradigm development, which supports the research of sustainable society, becomes a topic of study for scientists and organizations in these areas. The integration of industry and technology, as well as their implementation in social and economic development, is increasingly present in public administration and contributes to the same development of SIS. It is necessary to explore the balance between the development of sustainable use of the system and research, assuming the development of human consciousness, a higher degree of adaptation to the challenges arising from exponential growth and development of ICT, and is therefore part of the solution that brings sustainability, IO, growth and development. Researchers should consider different examples of interoperability and standardization, eg from aviation, with built-in levels and interoperability functions, as well as high-tech industry processes etc. When it comes to public administration challenges, additional efforts are needed as they need to provide further the development of standardization and alignment, due to factors of human behavior. By providing functional communication, standardization and interoperability, these systems should define goals, levels and optimum achieve full functional communication, with awareness of challenges in the absence of harmonization of development and sustainability.

7.6 Development of interoperability in the EU

The European Commission has established the European Frame of Interoperability (EIF). The European Semantic Interoperability Center (SEMIC.EU) has been launched in the last decade. Recent developments have shown that modern public administration systems in the EU affect weakly-connected components as a necessary infrastructure for the introduction of European public services in line with EIF 2.0. The significance of the political influence on national co-operation can be a challenge for EU member states because of free movement of workers, goods and services, etc. In the case of activities outside the EU, it is believed to initiate cooperation and national interoperability based on operational needs, but not on the same way as in the EU. This can not be substantiated based on the data collected, so the new data needs to be subjected to further living to determine what the co-operation supports. Being aware of these issues, political and scientific institutions and EU bodies have contributed to the establishment and development, and it is recommended to use the EIF as a framework for inter-state interoperable cooperation. This project is still under development, especially international interoperability. To ensure measurability and traceability for IO implementation, maturity levels are measured.

7.7 Interoperability development in the Republic of Croatia

Systems of interoperability in the Republic of Croatia are still under development and are strongly influenced by the EU. The same systems should ensure IS connectivity to a unique system for bridging legal, organizational, technical and semantic obstacles to the development of information infrastructure. The public register serves to build interoperable solutions and rationalize costs of information system development in the public sector by providing project control and decision-making on joint implementation of projects. The public register is also a function of a metric record with the function of the system development tool and the connection of public registers. The interoperability system developed and used in Croatia, in part, has GSB (Government Service Bus) features. The OIB system has been in use since 2009 and has a strong potential for establishing a single interoperability support system. This made it possible to create a unique identifier of the person. This is a legally accepted assumption for the exchange of information in the official records of the public law bodies.

The Republic of Croatia has launched the project "Strengthening Capacity for Better Public Administrations of the EU through the Transition Facility Transition Facility" to define the standards for linking and exchanging information and data between different state administration bodies, ie standards for determining the basis for safe data where the results are expected from the middle 2017. Interoperability is defined as a priority and each government has a program for establishing, developing and incorporating IO strategies, programs and implementations. One of the first complex issues is human resources, as the lack of qualified staff and appropriate education are accompanied by new values and priorities adopted by staff. These challenges are also present for private companies and for public administration and government. The EU has defined human resources critical, especially in the IT sector and in leading positions, because their support and adoption of new rules are key. Lack of experts and similar obstacles lead to limited results. There is another critical issue, which is the financing of such programs, as they usually last for decades, with a broad range of activities, with minimal short-term results and long-term results that are complex and almost inexplicable.

7.7.1 Developing interoperability - an example of EU and national agricultural administration and the possibility of case studies

As a new Member State, the Republic of Croatia has adopted the legal, political and economic framework of the EU as well as certain requirements to ensure inter-institutional interoperability. As the EU's total budget allocated to agriculture is allocated, specific policies, measures, strategies, programs, projects and other activities in the implementation of the Common Agricultural Policy have been developed. One of the IT systems in the Common Agricultural Policy of the EU as the horizontal policy instrument is the ISAMM - Information System for managing and monitoring the agricultural products market. The system is planned at the beginning of last decade and began with implementation in 2009. The role is primarily communicative but provides far more than the communication roles. It ensures inter-institutional interaction between systems and systems development and communication with other related systems.

A successful example of interinstitutional communication and coordination is the implementation of the ISAMM system, as it includes Member States with ministries, IT agencies, platforms such as AWAI, ECAS, CIRCA BC, as well as EUROSTAT and other EU systems to ensure communication, statistical, economic and other tasks, as part of the ZPP (Common Agricultural Policy) and ZOT (Joint Market Organizations) functionality. The EU has started implementing the ISAMM system in 2009 with a number of improvements through continuous development. Public institutions, as one of the leaders of social and economic development, are intensely following and introducing this practice, and science thus gets a new field for research.

8 Legal, ethical and socio-cultural aspects of the research proposal

As one of the basic features and basic functions of the BCT is its distributed P2P nature, each node in the network that has a full copy of the transaction. The same characteristics can have positive impacts and benefits in public administration. Although numerous authors have highlighted the benefits of using the BCT, these promises are made to be true, and no realization is guaranteed. If we include these conditions in interoperability systems, associated with appropriate business architecture, we open up space for new development and synergies through the concept of inter-institutional interoperability, which, under the assumptions of preparation and the appropriate conditions, as in the case of BCT, could provide easier transformation processes in public administration, as one of the leaders of social development, but also the stakeholders and users of the mentioned technologies and the key area of their application.

Namely, with the necessary changes in the legal framework, which does not yet support these changes of difficult scale, it is necessary to take into account the fact and how often are two different paradigms and value systems. On the one hand, we have a public administration, which processes and systems monitor, manage, communicate and coordinate the systems, which are difficult to harmonize and have a number of intermediaries and conditions, and on the other hand BCT is devolved to decentralization, democratization and management through consensus and standardization of standardized values, so called. adding "blocks" to the whole, the greater the challenge of aligning all these values and approaches. Interoperability in these conditions is "sine qua non" because large systems have to be synchronized through a series of components. Apart from the architecture, the legal and the political framework, it is also necessary to prepare and apply both BCT and the elementary components of ICT, software and applications, which are increasingly changing and conditioning new, organizational, technical and technological solutions.

The changes that new technologies allow and announce but also seek in the part of the system and the wider digital community mean adopting values and standards, transparency, paradigm shift on multiple levels and in different aspects. Therefore, this area, as regards interoperability, I3O concept and adoption of public administration development in new circumstances, should be explored through a series of future works, and this work intends to encourage research and development of the concept of interoperability in public administration, but also in all large and complex systems , de facto systems of group management systems and their mutual relationships, as a condition for further development, not just public administration and government, but also a viable information society whose components are already familiar and developed on a daily basis. In the practice so far, there has not been a systematic review of the benefits and weaknesses in the application of these new technologies, as development is accelerating rapidly, although new technologies are changing, while many values and characteristics are not supported by argumentative or empirical evidence.

The potential advantages and benefits of announcement may be numerous, but their complexity, interaction, dependence and dependence on decisions, design, architecture, as well as difficult predictable future application development have to be remembered. The basic benefits are recognized in the possible improvement and development of data integrity, transaction indepen- dence, monitoring capabilities, and transparency, which will surely help in the implementation of a number of anti-corruption programs and more and more complex and fraudulent frauds.

Due to weaknesses, challenges and inconsistencies, distributed solutions (such as BCT) are often less efficient than traditional centralized database solutions, scaling to larger capacity is very difficult and even more difficult to modify, leading to less flexibility and constraints in communications, which is often the case with open, public BCs like Bitcoin, where most of the users are conditioned by the support of future development and lack of room for their own contribution.

In the future use of information and application of new technologies, it is expected to increase and improve the reliability of information through the use of consensus mechanisms, which ensures data changes only with the stacking of all relevant parties, thus enhancing security in the distribution of books that are more difficult to manipulate. Additionally, design selection indicates the anonymity or public availability of the user, which is a critical component for all governments and public administrations. In line with the new trends and legislation (GDPR) and application development, which devoted particular attention to the issue of identity management, control and development of an identity management system, practiced by virtually all governments and public administrations, this area is increasingly challenging. The question is often asked - are key users and those who need to have the key?

In the case of transparency and possible impact on the reduction of corruption and fraud, it is difficult to accept some new technologies such as BCT as a driver or even as catalysts of the process, since they can not prevent malversations in providing social services, which requires changes in the systems themselves. Even the announcements that technology can build additional trust and how it is easier to monitor controls and audits, this claim is not easy to prove, as there is also a lack of research and materials that could confirm it with greater confidence. Announcements on reducing energy burdens also stem from a series of idealization and non-critical considerations, especially if one takes into account the fact that by introducing more nodes, the energy issue could become even more challenging. Of the many potential benefits and benefits attributed to BCT, some are necessary for significant changes in organizations, architecture, practices, both at the micro level within the institution and in a number of existing inter-organizational relationships, irrespective of the possible links to the I3O concept, so it is justified question how many advantages (or fulfilling the conditions for their achievement) actually outweigh the potential risks in the application.

BCT, I3O, interoperability and new technologies and architecture, depend on management, harmonized value systems, social development and ethical standards, and the institutional context is additionally updated. In addition to social development, feedback and feedback processes, both in government and public administrations, as well as the general public, there is a need for better quality evaluation to provide the appropriate approach and concept with the expected outcomes and outcomes. Public administration and government expect changes, both in organization, structure, and fulfillment of social requirements as key fucitities, such as equal access, transparency, accountability and privacy. In addition to development issues, there is also a question of specificity, recognizable for the concept, both in terms of interoperability and I3O concept. As with BCT, the challenge of defining specific advantages has been highlighted by constraints such as scalability, flexibility and response time.

9 Conclusions

9.1 Challenge of interoperability
Society, culture, markets, organizations, technology, science, groups, and individuals are undergoing turbulence with unpredictable intensity and consequences, so we witness changes to numerous paradigms. The growing impact of IT has surpassed expectations and the digital present indicates a more complex and demanding future for every aspect of human life. Complex systems and networks are becoming more complex, potentially improving every aspect and functionality, seeking multiple different approaches and methodologies, continually and dramatically redirecting and redefining organizations in almost every aspect, emphasizing the role of synergy, communication and IO. This complexity was enriched by networking and enterprise integration, business information systems, so interoperability became a "sine qua non" condition. Enterprises are focused on a viable IO to ensure compliance, functionality, development and sustainability. This is highlighted by the ever-increasing, dynamic and continuous changes in existing technology and the development of new ones. Changes in

technology generations outstripped their capabilities, especially because of the overall multiplication of knowledge, more and more often, until recently in a few decades and soon in annual cycles.

Technology adapted to the new reality more innovative and advanced, in the next two or three years in some areas, software, hardware and all components must adapt to turbulent changes, recognizing changes, with deeper impact and consequences. The author wants to support this new paradigm that will ensure optimum definition and application of resources and enable continuous access to communication and solutions to multiple IO challenges. New business systems condition sustainability, thereby supporting the development of a sustainable information society.

9.2 Conclusion and guidelines for further activities

E-government as one of the first tools for achieving a common platform and information system for various public administration schemes has established IO programs and secured different levels of awareness through various programs. Further development, adoption and implementation of new ICT and technological development is expected to ensure the strengthening of public administration. New e-Government models are focused on system integration, vertical and horizontal activities, including collaboration between institutions at different levels and platforms. IO enables collaboration and integration at national and national level. When considering new EU member states, such as Croatia, Hungary, the Czech Republic and Poland, the EU invests further efforts to support the development of IO management and development, especially in the past decade (Göte, 2009). These societies are described as transitional societies, contributing to the further development of the EU. (Ziemba, 2017)

The author aims to support and describe the I3O and public administration development, considering their interaction and benefits, believing that work would contribute to and support the new paradigm. Following the mentioned papers, research and related activities, the author proposes the development of the I3O concept - inter-institutional interoperability (the I3O concept supports and allows the development of a concept of culture of interoperability, which will also contribute to public administration with a significant impact on society and the economy.

The concept of behavioral economics and societal trends, future EA and IO issues will largely depend on human resources and behavioral factors, contributing to future public administration development and other large and complex systems, so ensuring internal and external organizational development, as well as necessary adaptation to a changing environment. As with IO, there are models and levels that describe evolution from initial awareness to systematically developed programs at the national level. The same systems include: (0) awareness, (1) introduction, (2) application and (3) adding value.

It also focuses on IO, including entity compatibility, procedures and equipment. In order to achieve the desired level of interoperability, IT systems and procedures for each component should have a minimum planned level of compatibility planned. Since IO has became one of the strategic topics in the EU, an increasing number of governments and institutions support solutions established and implemented to ensure e-government as a guideline for the new system and changes in public administration. In BCT, software and algorithms have to be revised to ensure its proper functioning and to analyze compliance with the rules.

This changed nature of audit procedures needs to be investigated due to its consequences in the institutional environment of auditing services and related actors. The software embedded algorithms determine whether the rules are met and the transactions are correct. Expectations from new technologies are focused on direct communication, improvement and development of interaction between citizens, providing opportunities for the public administration functioning and administration without public - government administrators, by governments' provided services. Basically, the concept of BCT replaces the intermediary through technology, because with the BCT there is no central body or third party in charge of processing, authorizing, certifying and approving the transaction, so there is no central bank managing currency for example.

In many situations, it has the function of controllers, monitors, updating and managing all registers. In this way, BCT could reduce or exclude the functionality of government roles and registers by storing official records and securing certain data. Yet, somebody still manages the entire system, functionality, design, maintenance, etc. The hardware and location issues, resource management, control are very sensitive ones, because the risk of role changes and proportions of political power are not excluded, so the influence or role of management becomes exposed to various risks. Accordingly, it is extremely important precisely for the sensitive nature of the political influence and power issues through this architecture, to ensure its infrastructure and management, which will ensure the continuity of information quality, as well as the stability of management, development and maintenance.

In the future government and public administration BCT implementation, governments and national administrations can play the administrator role who can, with some security mechanisms, provide a reliable way to initiate, establish, apply and maintain a register, by establishing, monitoring and checking transaction rules, as needed, and application audits, to ensure continuity of quality and functionality. By assuring the role of a data trustee, the role of the government is becoming more complex and more responsible because it takes responsibility for managing applications and is responsible for possible failures or data quality, and it is also necessary to re-intermediate government roles and the ability to develop and change roles.

Such opportunities and development should certainly be explored in practice and through several studies into critical areas for possible application of BCT. In order to reduce the expectations of the BCT, especially with regard to the so-called "decentralization and democratization process of public administration, it is necessary to point out that the BC requirements and the design itself have been set up by experts with limited responsibility for design decisions. Although in the case of BCT it is arguing about the data democratization, it is possible to reverse the scenarios. Those same experts who define and shape the system represent a minority they dictate the rules in which an application manages users. Having control and power, it is not excluded that your ambitions can focus on monetization and mere profit. Only an appropriate combination can change the code and affect the management of the system. Design will probably reflect the interests of all participants.

Although BCT is useful for supporting different values, its implementation is a sensitive issue, and the values reflect design choice. Therefore, BCT support critical and sensitive decision-making, especially in the situations of conditioning the decisions by consensus, but also the issue of governance becomes a stumbling block, since the avoidance of the mediator, the manager, as one of the thoughts of the guideline for building and applying BCT comes into question through application within major political government systems and public administration. On the other hand, the introduction of BCT into the system itself is not feasible without an appropriate analysis, data, harmonization, standardization and series of research to ensure clear terms, definitions and guidelines, implementing, and developing BCT in public administration. Decision making and public policy in this case must be a particularly delicate and careful process, assuming the maximum preparation, the appropriate information and background, as it is about managing decisions and policies, as well as processes and functionalities of governments and public administrations. Along with the above-mentioned fences and risks, that may ensure easier decision-making motivation, improved functionality and process management outcomes, possibly with the advancement of international co-operation.

As a guideline for further interoperability concept research, author would like to suggest set of multidisciplinary researches on defining the paradigm, construct of institutional and inter-institutional interoperability, developing new solutions and exploring them. As a key issue author has considered the challenges such as lack of quality information and research to analyze new technologies and approaches in terms of interoperability, legal and political frameworks, as well as new solutions and technologies introduction. Such a lack of information may be solved by conducting research, relevant data analysis and model findings, research proposals and problem solving. Assuming the institutional acceptance of the paradigm shift, research introduction as an entering at the small door, the most of governments and public administrations, who invest significant resources into new technologies, are working on research of all those areas.

In addition to strategy analysis, the introduction of new strategies and programs, interoperability, cross-border and regional cooperation, there are respectable funds also provided to improve the institutional framework, architecture and new system solutions. Interoperability and new technologies provided their contribution in many ways, but require precautions and additional research to ensure the evaluation of these solutions, but also to secure new findings and new scientific contributions. New technologies appear in numerous and various different shapes, featuring different properties. For BCT, the key topics are private or public closed BCs (referred to as Private / Publicly Allowed BCs), based on the level of openness and allocation of permits. In the case of BCT, control has owners and only they have the ability to provide access to and assign new nodes to BC architecture. When private BC is set up, a permitted network is built in which participants need permission to access the network. Nevertheless, government organizations may also decide to develop a public BC, which the public can observe and mutate under the conditions set by a government organization.

The new role of users in such applications transition depends on their reading and writing rights. Some users can only read the data while others will make the data by doing the transactions. In permitted BCs, only subscribers can add new blocks and transactions to the BC. This implies that node operators in BC imitate BC architect. Only trusted organizations can manage a node and be involved in the consensus creation process to add new data blocks. Operators may be limited to public organizations, but this reflects the choice of design. Governments must choose the most appropriate approach and the BCT, due to a number of the above conditions and benefits, but also a compromise, and the issue of control and ownership of data still poses a challenge in the relationships of stakeholders to this great potential social project. Control, ownership of data, privacy and access are key decisions. The more control, the BC system will less resemble the original BC vision.

Such an application may be open to all or limited in some elements such as voting and access to data. In an open access to information, users can view all information that can cause serious privacy issues, personal or other sensitive information stored in BC, then access should only be approved when the conditions set out in the Privacy Policy were met. This requires encryption and access control. For this purpose BC can combine with other technologies such as encryption and business rules. The General Data Protection Regulation (GDPR) (Regulation (EU) 2016/679) is a regulation by which the European Parliament, the Council of the European Union and the European Commission intend to strengthen and unify data protection for all individuals within the European Union (EU). In these cases, the BC requirement should be able to meet these requirements. The number of experiments with BCT executed by individual governments is on the rise and a good example has been given by the Netherlands (eg: https://www.blockchainpilots.nl/). Such experiments use different technologies and software. Since this divergent strategy is needed to find useful applications and technologies, this could result in fragmented and duplicate efforts over a longer period of time. Therefore, experimentation must lead to standardization in order to converge to a common standard. Ølnes and Jansen (2017) call on the BCT platform to run various e-government applications. Such a common infrastructure avoids the development of new infrastructure. There remain open questions as to who controls technology and whether requirements from the legislative environment are met.

The new society, increasingly influenced by ICT, control of information, technology and networks, provides additional power and influence over society. BCT supports information infrastructure, so is potentially important as a future infrastructure for open innovation. There are a growing number of governments and companies that encourage innovation. Governments can become a shared BC provider using infrastructure that enables public authorities, ministries and bodies to create BC applications, so to ensure safe BCT and reliable legislation implementation. Technology and data standardization are needed for interoperability. Despite the attractiveness and growing popularity of BCT, their distribution, decentralization and design require a number of changes in the area of responsibility, control and management approaches. The implementation of new technologies can take and vary in different shapes, resulting in different benefits. BC implementations are largely technology-based and often require different technology combinations to make BC architecture suitable for e-government applications.

Transactions may be stored in BC and document data in another system that transactions relate to. For e-government domain applications, institutional aspects play an important role, so need to be taken into account when using BCT. Alike to the cloud issues, there will probably be discussion of the geographic position of servers and nodes. Some governments require that geographically located servers are within their jurisdiction due to the application of different laws. Many solutions can be controlled by technology rather than social problems that need to be solved. BCT advocates technology as the key to solving virtually all problems, but in practice it is a tough challenge. A technology-based solution can be interpreted with immature technology and limited knowledge of the potential of the technology itself. In the process of maturing, it is necessary to develop technology geared to the needs of society, which includes social issues and public values, and BC architecture and e-government applications should be developed in line with new management models.

Considering new technologies and systems implementation, we have to be aware that there is no single solution and such a process is not a linear, rational or deterministic. It opens space for uncertain outputs and outcome, therefore additional experimentation is needed to understand technology features and constraints. New technologies application often results in a human behavior change with reversal effect on the same applications, creating a kind of spiral with an indefinite outcome. Such an experimentation need additional space for application changes in technical way, as well as adaptations to changing circumstances. Accordingly, there is a need for adaptability as a critical success factor for ICT systems, so it is not yet clear how the BCT will fit into adaptation in public administration. Additionally, any implementation largely requires some level of standardization to ensure interoperability.

As a conclusion and further guidance, the paper opened area for various possible research projects as a continuation or link to the already started and proposed researches in the field of interoperability, implementation of new technologies and innovations.

References

Agostinho, C., Ducq, Y., Zacharewicz, G., Sarraipa, J., Lampathaki, F., Poler, R., Jardim-Goncalves R., (2016) Towards a sustainable interoperability in networked enterprise information systems: Trends of knowledge and model-driven technology, On Next Generation Enterprise Information Systems, 79, pp.64 - 76. HAL Id: hal-01387821 https://hal.archives-ouvertes.fr/hal-01387821

ATHENA. (2003) Advanced Technologies for Interoperability of Heterogeneous Enterprise Networks and their Applications, FP6-2002-IST1, Integrated Project Proposal

Bakar, N. A., Harihodin, S., Nazri K., (2016), Assessment of Enterprise Architecture Implementation Capability and Priority in Public Sector Agency Conference on ENTERprise Information Systems / International Conference on Project Management / Conference on Health and Social Care Information Systems and Technologies, CENTERIS / ProjMAN / HCist, Kuala Lumpur, Malaysia 2016

C3 Technical Architecture (NC3TA), (2003) NATO Allied Data Publication 34 (ADatP-34), NATO C3 Technical Architecture (NC3TA), Version 4.0.

C4ISR Interoperability Working Group, (1998) Levels of information systems interoperability (LISI), Tech. report, US Department of Defense, Washington, DC, USA

CEN/ISO standardization process - https://www.cencenelec.eu/intcoop/StandardizationOrg/Pages/default.aspx

Central State Administrative Office for e-Croatia (2010): e-Croatia Implementation Plan for Year 2008, available at http://e-hrvatska.hr/sdu/hr/ Program E- Hrvatska/Provedba/StrategijeI Programi / categoryParaGraph /01113/ document/ Plan_ provedbe_Programa _e_Hrvatska _za_2008 .pdf, Croatia Retrieved 04/04/ 2016

Chapman R. E. (2005) Inadequate Interoperability: A Closer Look at the Costs 22nd International Symposium on Automation and Robotics in Construction, ISARC 2005 – Ferrara, Italy, 2005 http://www.nist.gov/manuscript-publication Retrieved 07/04/2016

Chen, D., Doumeingts, G., (2003) European initiatives to develop interoperability of enterprise applications - basic concepts, framework and roadmap Annual Reviews in Control 27, University Bordeaux, 2003

Chen D., Doumeingts G., Vernadat F. (2008) Architectures for Enterprise Integration and Interoperability: Past, Present and Future, In: Special issue on Enterprise Integration and Interoperability in Manufacturing Systems, A. Molina and H. Panetto (Eds). Elsevier Computers In Industry, 59/5, USA

Chesbrough, H., Open Innovation Definition, (2003), https://www.innoget.com/open-innovation-definition

Cretan, A., Coutinho, C., Bratu, B., Jardim-Goncalves R. (2012) NEGOSEIO: A framework for negotiations toward Sustainable Enterprise Interoperability Proceedings of the 14th IFAC Symposium on Information Control Problems in Manufacturing Bucharest, Romania, May 23-25, 2012

De Vrande, V. V., De Jong J. P. J., Vanhaverbeke, W., de Rochemont, M. (2009), Open innovation in SMEs: Trends, motives and management challenges, Technovation 29 (2009) 423–437, www.elsevier.com/locate/technovation

Directive 2013/37/ EU (2013), of the European Parliament and of the Council amending Directive 2003/98/EC, on the re-use of public sector information. OJ L 175, p. 1.

Dolin, R. H., L., Alschuler, (2010) Approaching semantic interoperability in Health Level Seven, J Am Med Inform Assoc. 2011 Jan-Feb; 18(1): 99–103. Published online, The Journal of the American Medical Association (JAMIA) for biomedical and health informatics 2010 Nov 24. doi: 10.1136/jamia.2010.007864 , PMCID: PMC3005878

D'Elia, A., Viola, F., Roffia, L., Azzoni, P., Salmon Cinotti, T., (2017), Enabling Interoperability in the Internet of Things: A OSGi Semantic Information Broker Implementation International Journal on Semantic Web & Information Systems archive. Volume 13 Issue 1, January 2017, Pages 134-154, IGI Publishing Hershey, PA, USA, doi>10.4018/IJSWIS.2017010108

E-Business Watch (2011): Methodology, Available at http://www.ebusiness-watch.org/about/ methodology.htm - Retrieved 07/04/ 2016

Edvinsson, H., Aderinne, L., (2013), Enterprise Architecture Made Simple: Using the Ready, Set, Go Approach to Achieving Information Centricity Perfect Paperback – November 1, 2013

EIF - European Interoperability Framework (2004), for pan-European eGovernment Services, Interoperable Delivery of European eGovernment Services to public Administrations, Businesses and Citizens (IDABC), Luxembourg

European Commission Communication "EUROPE 2020" (2010) - A strategy for smart, sustainable and inclusive growth, COM - 2020 final. Retrieved 07/04/2016

Fuchs C. Sustainability and the information society. In: Berleur T, Numinen MI, Impagliazzo T, editors. IFIP International Federation for Information Processing, 223, Social informatics: an information society for all? In remembrance of Rob Kling; Boston: Springer; 2006; 219–230.

Fuchs C. The implications of new information and communication technologies for sustainability. Environ Dev Sustainability. 2008;10(3):291–309.

Galbraith, J.R. (2002), Organising to deliver solutions. Organizational Dynamics, Jay R. Galbraith, Centre for Effective Organizations, Marshall School of Business, University of Southern California, Los Angeles, USA

Gartner (2016), Gartner Glossary of Information Technology Acronyms and Terms, Edited by: Gartner 1-395, http://www.gartner.com/it-glossary/enterprise-resource-planning-erp/ Retrieved 08/04/2016

Gartner (2007a). IT's Role in a Low-Carbon Economy. Gartner, Inc. and/or its Affiliates.

Gartner (2007b). Green IT: A New Industry Shock Wave. Gartner, Inc. and/or its Affiliates.

Gartner (2008). Green IT – Where to Invest. Gartner, Inc. and/or its Affiliates.

Global eSustainability Initiative (2008). SMART 2020: Enabling the low carbon economy in the information age. Creative Commons 2008.

Green, P. F., (2005), Rosemann M., Indulska M., Ontological Evaluation of Enterprise Systems Interoperability Using ebXML Published in: Journal IEEE Transactions on Knowledge and Data Engineering archive Volume 17 Issue 5, May 2005 Page 713-725 IEEE Educational Activities Department Piscataway, NJ, USA doi>10.1109/TKDE.2005.79

Guedria, W., Naudet, Y., Chen, D., (2008), Interoperability maturity models - Survey & Comparison. In: Proc. of the 3rd IFAC/IFIP, OTM EI2N 2008 workshop, (Enterprise Integration, Interoperability and Networking), Monterrey, Mexico

Gøtze, J., Christiansen, P. E., Mortensen, R. K., Paszkowski, S. (2009), Cross-National Interoperability and Enterprise Architecture, Informatica. 2009, Vol. 20, Issue 3, p369-396. 28 p. 1, Copenhagen Business School, Denmark (2009), web-site accessed 8.10.2017.

Hajdin, G., Vrček, N. (2010) Methodologies for Measuring E-Government Development: The Croatian Case // Proceedings of the 21st Central European Conference on Information and Intelligent Systems /. Faculty of Organization and Informatics, Varaždin, Croatia, 319-325

Hemilä, J., (2002) Information technologies for value network integration, VTT Industrial Systems, VTT Technical Research Centre of Finland, Vuorimiehentie 5, VTT, Finland

Hilty, L.M., Aebischer, B.: ICT for Sustainability: An Emerging Research Field. In: Hilty, L.M., Aebischer, B. (eds.) ICT Innovations for Sustainability. Advances in Intelligent Systems and Computing. Springer, Heidelberg (2014)

Hinkelmann, K., Gerber, A., Karagiannis, D., Thönssen, B., Van der Merwe, A., Woitsch, R. (2016). A new paradigm for the continuous alignment of business and IT: Combining enterprise architecture modelling and enterprise ontology. Computers in Industry. Vol. 79, pp. 77-86. Available at: http://www.sciencedirect.com/science/article/pii/S0166361515300270.

IDABC - European Commission (2004): European Interoperability Framework for Pan-European E-government Services, Version 1.0 EIF European Interoperability Framework IDABC European – Version 1.0, Office for Official Publications of the European Communities, Luxembourg, 2004. http://ec.europa.eu/idabc/en /document/7841.html Retrieved 02/04/2016

Information Technology Vocabulary. ISO/IEC, (2013), Part 1: Fundamental terms www.iso.org /cate/d7229.html Retrieved 04/04/ 2016.

Interinstitutional Agreement (2013) between the European Parliament, the Council and the Commission on budgetary discipline, on cooperation in budgetary matters and on sound financial management OJ C 373, 20.12.2013, p. 1-11

INTEROP (2007), Enterprise Interoperability -Framework and knowledge corpus- Final report, INTEROP NOE, FP6 -Contact n 508011, Deliverable DI.3

Interop NOE (IST-2004-508011) (2004 to 2007), ATHENA "Advanced Technologies for Interoperability of Heterogeneous Enterprise Networks and their Application" (2007), IST-2004-507849) or R4eGov (IST-2004-026650). Germany. Retrieved 08/04/2016

Interoperability, Business dictionary, (2017), http://www.businessdictionary.com/definition/ interoperability.html

Interoperability (2007), Research for Networked Enterprises Applications and Software, FP6-IST 508011 (Interop NoE), http://www.interop-vlab.eu / Germany, Retrieved 08/04/2016

International Organization for Standardization Information technology -- Vocabulary https://www.iso.org/standard/7229.html Retrieved 08/04/2016

ISO (2006a). ISO 14040:2006, Environmental Management - Lifecycle Assessment - Principles and Framework. International Organization for Standardization.

ISO (2006b). ISO 14044:2006: Environmental Management - Lifecycle Assessment – Requirements and Guidelines. International Organization for Standardization.Janssen, M., Ubacht, J., Ølnes, S., (2017.), Blockchain in government: Benefits and implications of distributed ledger technology for information sharing, Government Information Quarterly 34 (2017) 355–364, ScienceDirect, pristup odobren ustupanjem autora: www.elsevier.com/locate/govinf, Netherlands, 2017, Pretraživanje Internet stranice 8.10.2017.

Lapalme, J., Gerber, A., Van der Merwe, A., Zachman, J., De Vries, M., Hinkelmann, K., (2015), Exploring the future of Enterprise Architecture: A Zachman Perspective, Computers in Industry 2015

Mansell, R. & Wehn, U. (Eds.) (1998). Knowledge Societies: Information Technology for Sustainable Development. Oxford: Oxford University Press. Retrieved April 24, 2006 from http://www.sussex.ac.uk/spru/1-4-9-1-1-2.html

Molina A., Panetto H., Chen D., Whitman L., Chapurlat V., Vernadat F.B., (2007), Enterprise Integration and Networking: Challenges and Trends. Studies in Informatics and Control, Informatics and Control Publications 353-368

Nishimura, T., Sakane, E., Yamaji, K., Nakamura, M., Aida, K., Klingenstein, N., (2016), Virtual organization platform interoperability provides the long tail an eScience environment National Institute of Informatics, Journal of Information Processing. (Journal of Information Processing, 2016, 24(4):609-619) Information Processing Society of Japan, 2016, ISSN: 18826652 03875806 DOI:

Nikpay F, Ahmad R, Yin Kia C., (2016), A hybrid method for evaluating enterprise architecture implementation. PUBMED 2017 Feb; 60:1-16. doi: 10.1016/j.evalprogplan.2016.09.001. Epub 2016

Niu, N., Xu, L. D., and Z. Bi, Enterprise Information Systems Architecture - Analysis and Evaluation, IEEE Transactions on Industrial Informatics, Vol. 9, No. 4, November 2013

Olsen, D. H., Trelsgård K., (2016) Enterprise Architecture adoption challenges: An exploratory case study of the Norwegian higher education sector. Department of Information Systems, University of Agder, Post box 422, N-4604 Kristiansand, Norway, Conference on ENTERprise Information Systems / International Conference on Project MANagement / Conference on Health and Social Care Information Systems and Technologies, CENTERIS / ProjMAN / HCist 2016, October 5-7, 2016

Panetto, H., Tursi, A., Morel, G., Dassisti, M., (2009), Ontological approach for productcentric information system interoperability in networked manufacturing enterprises, Annual Reviews in Control, Elsevier, 2009, 33 (2), pp. 238-245. DOI 10.1016/j.arcontrol.2009.05.003

Schmitz, P. Francesconi, E., Hajlaoui, N., Batouche B., (2017) Towards a Public Multilingual Knowledge Management Infrastructure for the European Digital Single Market, Publications Office of the European Union, Luxembourg, Luxembourg and ITTIG-CNR, Florence, Italy Towards a Public Multilingual Knowledge Management Infrastructure for the European Digital Single Market, 2017

Šimić, D., Vidović, S., (2011), Interoperability and Government Performance Management, 9th eeeGov|Days, Conf., 9-10 May 2011, Ljubljana, Slovenija, Pretraživanje Internet stranice 7.10.2017.

United Nations: United Nations e-Government Survey 2010, available at http://unpan1.un.org/intradoc/ groups/public/documents/UN-DPADM/ UNPAN038853.pdf, Accessed: March 2010.

Vernadat, F. B., (2009) Technical, Semantic and Organizational Issues of Enterprise Interoperability and Networking, Proceedings of the 13th IFAC Symposium on Information Control Problems in Manufacturing Moscow, Russia, June 3-5, 2009

Wu, B., Sixia,F., Junfang Yu A., Xi, L., (2016), Configuration and operation architecture for dynamic cellular manufacturing product–service system, Journal of Cleaner Production, ISSN: 0959-6526, Vol: 131, Page: 716-727 Elsevier BV

W3C – semantic web https://www.w3.org/standards/semanticweb/

Zachman J. (2008), The Official Concise Definition. Zachman International. 2008. The Zachman Framework Evolution. Zachman International. April 2009. Pretraživanje Internet stranice 7.10.2017.

Zhi-Gang Tao, Yun-Feng Luo, Chang-Xin Chen, Ming-Zhe Wang & Feng Ni (2015) Enterprise application architecture development based on DoDAF and TOGAF Pages 627-651 | Received 19 Mar 2014, Accepted 29 Jun 2015, Published online: 27 Jul 2015

Ziemann J. (2010), Architecture of Interoperable Information Systems. An Enterprise Model-Based Approach for Describing and Enacting Collaborative Business Processes, Wirtschafts-informatik - Theorie und Anwendung, Germany

Ziemba E. (2017), The Contribution of ICT Adoption to the Sustainable Information Society, Journal of Computer Information Systems http://www.tandfonline.com/toc/ucis20/current, Poland, 2017